water

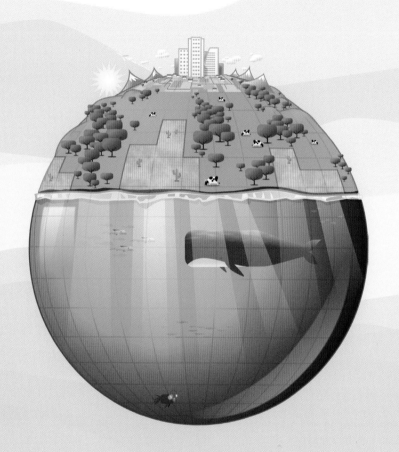

Written by Trevor Day

Series Consultant Dr Jon Woodcock

LONDON, NEW YORK, MELBOURNE,
MUNICH, AND DELHI

Senior editor Fran Jones
Senior art editors Smiljka Surla, Jacqui Swan
Editors Samone Bos, Sue Malyan, Andrea Mills
Art editors Sheila Collins, Phil Letsu
Managing editor Linda Esposito
Managing art editor Diane Thistlethwaite
Publishing manager Andrew Macintyre
Category publisher Laura Buller
Design development manager Sophia M Tampakopoulos
Picture research Liz Moore
DK picture library Claire Bowers
Production controller Erica Rosen
DTP designer Andy Hilliard
Jacket editor Mariza O'Keeffe
Jacket designers Jacqui Swan, Smiljka Surla

Illustrations Dave Cockburn

First published in Great Britain in 2007 by
Dorling Kindersley Limited,
80 Strand,
London WC2R 0RL

2 4 6 8 10 9 7 5 3
TDA043 – 12/06

ISBN: 978-1-40531-874-7

Jacket colour reproduction by Colourscan, Singapore
Inside colour reproduction by Wyndeham pre-press, London
Printed and bound in China by Hung Hing

**Discover more at
www.dk.com**

contents

Wet stuff (H₂O)

Water is the most common – and most remarkable – substance on Earth's surface. It is also the only matter that is naturally abundant as a solid, a liquid, and a gas. The smallest amount of water that exists is a water molecule, which is made up of two atoms of hydrogen (H_2) and one of oxygen (O) bonded tightly together. A drop of water contains more than one billion, billion water molecules.

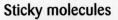

Sticky molecules

The hydrogen atoms in a water molecule are slightly positively charged electrically and the oxygen atom is slightly negative. Opposite charges attract, so water molecules tend to "stick" together.

Surface tension

When water molecules stick together across the surface of water, they form a "skin" on the water. This effect is called surface tension. Water's surface tension can support the weight of insects, such as this pond skater.

Water as a solid

When water freezes, its molecules slow down and huddle together. Each molecule links with four others and pulls into an arrangement of interconnected rings. Ice is hard because the water molecules are locked into this crystal pattern.

Water as a liquid

In liquid water, the water molecules are only loosely connected by electrical attractions, and the molecules are free to move around. This is why liquid water flows easily when poured and takes on the shape of its container.

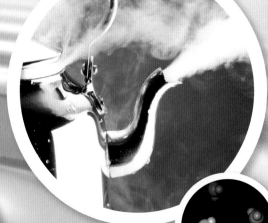

Water as a gas

In steam, the water molecules have too much energy and move too quickly for electrical attractions to hold them together. So steam has no shape – it just expands to fill the available space.

Water in space
The electrical forces between water molecules naturally pull them inwards to form spheres. In space there is hardly any gravity, so water drops float. Here, an astronaut is visible through a perfectly spherical drop of water, which is acting as a lens.

Water and gravity
This water drop is being pulled off a leaf by gravity. As the drop falls, it will become almost spherical in shape. Then air pushing against it will squash it into a bun shape, or it might split into several droplets.

Universal solvent
Sugar, salt, and soluble aspirin are just a few of the things that dissolve in water. In fact, more chemicals dissolve in water than in any other liquid. This is because the electrical charges on water molecules attract the atoms from other substances. This pulls the substances apart and drags them into a solution.

Water facts		
Freezes At sea level, pure water will freeze at a temperature of 0°C (32°F).	**Boils** At sea level, pure water will boil at a temperature of 100°C (212°F).	**Expands** Water is unusual because it expands when it freezes. Other liquids get smaller.
Salty If water has salt dissolved in it, then it has a lower freezing point and a higher boiling point.	**Fresh** Pure water in a glass tumbler has no smell, no colour, and no taste.	**Impure** Water dissolves substances well, so when it flows through soil or rock, chemicals get picked up.
Burns Burning produces water. When most substances burn in air, they release steam.	**Melts** When ice melts, it absorbs heat energy. This is why ice is good for cooling drinks.	**Altitude** At high altitude, pure water boils at the lower temperature of 86°C (186°F).

Water world

Water world

The blue planet
In photos taken from space, the Earth appears mostly blue, because of the huge areas of ocean. The white swirls are clouds containing water in the form of droplets and ice crystals.

Planet Earth is a watery place, with more than 70 per cent of its surface covered in seawater. Most of this water is found in five oceans – giant hollows that have filled with salty water. Of the remaining surface water, most is locked up in ice around the North and South Poles. The water in lakes, rivers, clouds, soils, and living organisms is small by comparison, but very important.

Light penetration

0

5 m (16 ft)

10 m (32 ft)

100 m (326 ft)

Depth of ocean

The first oceans
Scientists think that the first oceans formed nearly 4 billion years ago. The ocean water probably came from steam, which was released by erupting volcanoes. The steam cooled and turned to water in the atmosphere, then fell to Earth as rain. This collected in low-lying areas to create oceans.

Why is the sea blue?
Water is slightly blue, but this is only obvious when you see it in large amounts, and when the water is not stained by particles, such as sand or mud. Clear seawater in bright sunshine, as around this coral atoll, looks a rich blue because the water has absorbed other colours in the light.

Absorbing light
Sunlight contains all the colours of the rainbow, but water absorbs some colours of light more than others. Water absorbs colours at the red end of the spectrum much better than those at the blue-green end, which penetrate much deeper.

Light underwater
Even the most beautiful, multi-coloured coral reefs can look quite drab underwater. Everything looks very blue-green because the water filters out red and yellow light. However, if you shine a beam of white light underwater the full range of colours is magically revealed.

Clouds
Just 0.001% of surface water is contained in the atmosphere, some of it in clouds.

Living organisms
A minute 0.00004% of water on Earth's surface is found in living organisms.

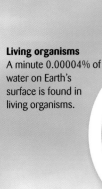

Rivers, lakes, and groundwater
About 0.7% of Earth's surface water is in rivers, lakes, soil, and shallow rocks.

Oceans
A massive 97.2% of all surface water lies in the oceans.

Ice caps and glaciers
About 2.1% of surface water is found in the frozen ice caps and in glaciers.

Water on Earth's surface
If all the land areas, water, and ice on Earth's surface were grouped together, this is how our planet might look. More than two-thirds of the surface is covered in liquid water. About half of the ice sits on the land, and half floats on the sea.

Salty or fresh

Anyone who has swallowed seawater while swimming knows it tastes salty. In fact, most of the liquid water on Earth's surface lies in the oceans. The salt, called sodium chloride, comes from soil and rocks on the land. Over millions of years, rivers have gradually washed this salt into the sea. Fresh water is found in most lakes and rivers, locked up as ice, and in the atmosphere. It contains very little dissolved salt. Seawater is not safe for people to drink, but fresh water – providing it lacks harmful chemicals or microbes – is safe to swallow.

TF	Tropical fresh water
F	Fresh water
T	Tropical seawater
S	Summer (temperate) seawater
W	Winter (temperate) seawater

Staying afloat

An object's ability to float in water is known as buoyancy. Water provides more buoyancy when it contains dissolved salt or other substances. The symbol above, called a Plimsoll line, is used on cargo ships and marks the level to which the ship can be safely loaded. The maximum load in seawater (T) would cause the ship to sink a bit lower if it sailed into fresh water (F). Warm water provides even less buoyancy so the boat would sink further (TF).

Fresh water

At the start of a river, the fresh water it contains is usually clean and clear. As it gradually flows through the landscape, the river picks up more sediment and dissolved substances.

Estuaries

The place where a river meets the sea is called an estuary. Here, fresh water and seawater mix. Water in estuaries is brackish – saltier than fresh water, but not as salty as seawater.

Oceans

The oceans are salty because the water in them is constantly evaporating into the air, leaving salts behind. Some inland lakes have no outflows and can become salty too.

Salt of the Earth

If all the water in the oceans evaporated, and the salt that remained was piled onto the land, it would form a layer more than 120 m (400 ft) deep. This is so much salt that it could cover the land with salt buildings that averaged 30 storeys high.

Salty lake

The Dead Sea is a lake between Israel and Jordan. It contains the world's saltiest water – nine times saltier than seawater. Swimmers in the Dead Sea are very buoyant and float easily.

Valuable salt

Here in Vietnam, the Sun's heat is being used to evaporate the water from seawater in artificial ponds. Salt from the seawater is left behind and people gather it up to sell.

pH scale

Acids and alkalis are chemicals that can cause strong reactions. Strong acids and alkalis can "burn" skin. The pH scale is used to show how strong an acid or alkali is. Pure water is neutral – neither acid nor alkali. It lies in the middle of the scale with a pH of 7.

pH SCALE

Extremely acidic

Neutral

Extremely alkaline

	0
Battery acid, sulphuric acid	1
Lemon juice, vinegar	2
Orange juice, fizzy drinks, wine	3
Acid rain, tomatoes, beer	4
Bananas, black coffee	5
Rainwater, milk, urine	6
Pure water, blood	7
Seawater, eggs	8
Soap	9
Milk of magnesia, detergents	10
Ammonia, household cleaners	11
Baking soda	12
Laundry bleach	13
Strong drain bleach	14

Frozen water

Ice forms in the coldest parts of the planet – especially around the North and South Poles and on mountain peaks. As we see from ice cubes in a glass, ice floats on water. If it didn't, the polar oceans would freeze solid, from the bottom up. The ice on top acts like a blanket, slowing the cooling of the water below. More than three-quarters of all fresh water on Earth's surface is ice – about half lying on the land and the other half floating on the sea.

Why ice floats
When water gets close to freezing point, the molecules in it move slightly further apart as they start to form crystals. As a result, freezing water contains fewer molecules than warmer water, so it is lighter. This is why ice and near-frozen water always float on top of warmer water.

Iceberg
An iceberg is a giant chunk of freshwater ice that has broken away from a glacier or ice sheet and floated out to sea. This process of breaking away is called calving. In a typical iceberg, less than 20 per cent of the ice can be seen above the surface of the water.

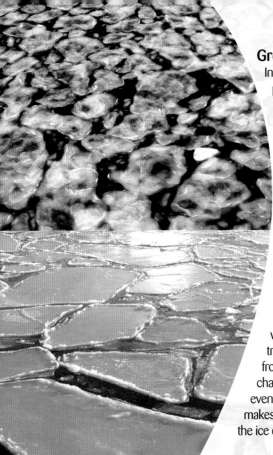

Grease ice

In winter, the seawater in the polar regions freezes, creating vast areas of ice. When sea ice begins to form, ice crystals gather at the sea surface. The winds and waves keep these crystals in small clumps. This thin ice looks like fat floating on the sea and is called grease ice.

Pancake ice

As grease ice thickens and is shaped by the wind and waves, it breaks up into "pancakes" of ice with turned-up edges. Ice crystals trap little or no salt, so the salt from the seawater is pushed into channels inside the ice and eventually trickles out. This makes the seawater under the ice even saltier.

Snowflakes

When the air is cold, ice crystals grow around specks of dust inside clouds to form snowflakes. When they are large and heavy enough, the flakes fall. Each snowflake contains 50 or more ice crystals, arranged in a unique six-sided pattern. No two are identical.

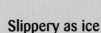

Slippery as ice

This skater is actually skating on a thin layer of liquid water, just a few molecules thick, which forms on top of the ice under the blades of his skates. When he moves on, the liquid layer instantly freezes back into ice. Scientists still disagree about exactly how this layer forms.

Sea-ice sheets

Pancake ice usually freezes to form a continuous sheet of ice, which is about 1 m (3 ft) thick in its first year. Each winter, huge sheets of sea ice grow southwards in the Arctic Ocean and northwards in the Southern Ocean around Antarctica.

Ice floes

Sheets of sea ice up to 10 km (6 miles) across are called floes; larger sheets of ice are known as ice fields. Many of the floes break up during the summer months when the weather warms up. Winds, waves, and currents make the floes jostle about and help to break them up more quickly.

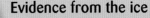

Evidence from the ice

An ice core is a column of ice drilled out of a glacier or an ice sheet. The ice contains air and particles of dust and pollen that were trapped in it hundreds, or thousands, of years ago. When analyzed, the air reveals the balance of gases in the atmosphere at that time. The dust and pollen give scientists valuable clues about the climate long ago.

Tree of life

During the wet season, this baobab tree in Africa stores water to help it survive the dry season. Spongy fibres inside the tree's trunk swell up to store more than 100,000 litres (22,000 gal) of water, which locals can use if there is a drought.

Solid wood

The wood inside a tree trunk is made of thousands of water-transporting vessels. The walls of these vessels are lined with a tough substance called lignin, which gives wood its immense strength. Each tree "ring" represents a year's growth.

In leaves, water is used to manufacture food using sunlight (photosynthesis).

Water evaporates into the air from pores on the bottom of leaves.

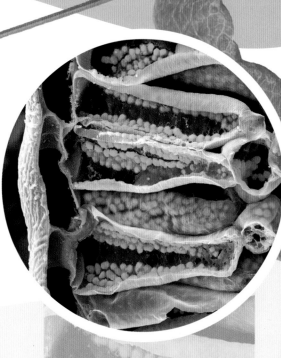

Open pore

Leaves have pores called stomata (singular stoma) on their underside. They open and close to control the loss of water from the leaf. The stoma shown here is open. This allows the gas carbon dioxide, which the plant needs for photosynthesis, to enter the leaf from the air. At the same time, water exits the leaf through the pore.

Leaf factor

This section through the top of a leaf shows a group of highly magnified cells. The flattened cells at the top have a waxy coating on their upper surface, which prevents water escaping. Photosynthesis occurs inside structures called chloroplasts. These are shown as false-coloured green blobs inside the long cells.

Water and plants

Transpiration

Water evaporates from the surface of cells inside leaves and passes out through pores into the air. This loss of water is called transpiration. The process helps the plant by "pulling" water and nutrients through it. However, if transpired water cannot be replaced with more water from the soil, the plant soon wilts.

Microscopic vessels in the stem transport water up to the leaves.

The main root carries water up into the stem.

Small roots take up water and nutrients from the soil.

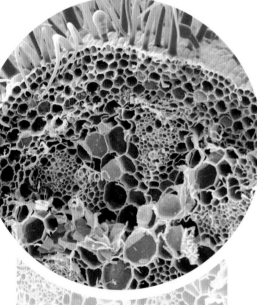

Water transporter

The inside of a plant stem is packed with thousands of tiny tubes called vessels. They are made from cells that connect end to end then die, leaving a hollow tube. In these thin tubes, surface tension works to pull water up the stem. This is known as capillary action.

Root hairs

Smaller roots, such as the ones on these seedlings, are covered with hundreds of tiny outgrowths called root hairs. They create a huge surface area for absorbing water. Each root hair is only about 0.1 mm (0.003 in) wide and is covered in a single layer of cells so that it can swiftly take up water and nutrients from the soil.

Plants operate like mini-factories, carrying out all sorts of processes – and they need water for all of them. Water transports substances around the plant, in the same way that blood moves through a person's body. All the plant's chemical reactions, such as making food using sunlight (photosynthesis), take place in water. This water is absorbed from the ground through the roots and makes up at least 80 per cent of every plant. Water pressure keeps the plant's stem and leaves well supported.

Life in water

Scientists think that the first life forms may have evolved at the edges of the oceans more than 3.5 billion years ago. Today, most water teems with life, from microscopic plankton to the largest whale. For each, the water affects its shape and how it lives. As water is hundreds of times heavier and thicker than air, it supports organisms more readily than air does. However, water offers more resistance to movement, so large marine animals have a streamlined shape to help them slip easily through water.

Plant plankton

These rings are chalky plates in the skeleton of a coccolithophorid. This minute organism is a type of plant plankton (phytoplankton) and is 10 times smaller than a full stop. Being so tiny, it sinks very slowly and does not have to swim hard to stay afloat near the water surface.

Animal plankton

This is the skeleton of a radiolarian, a tiny animal plankton (zooplankton). It eats smaller organisms, such as coccolithophorids. The spikes enlarge its surface area and increase friction with the water, which helps it to float. Many types of radiolarian contain oil droplets or air bubbles that help them stay afloat.

Algal blooms

There are so many phytoplankton in the sea that they can form great green patches, called algal blooms. The turquoise areas here are phytoplankton in the North Sea, off Scandinavia. These populations perform the same function that forests do on land. They take in carbon dioxide and give out oxygen in the process of photosynthesis, refreshing the Earth's atmosphere.

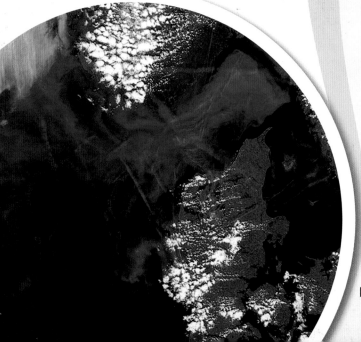

Bony fish

These fast-swimming tuna are highly streamlined to help them cut through the water. A tuna breathes in water and takes oxygen from it using its gills, which are hidden behind a flap at each side of its head. An air sac inside its body buoys the fish up. Tuna find prey using sensitive cells along the flanks that detect vibrations in the water.

Cartilaginous fish

With a skeleton of light cartilage (gristle) rather than heavy bone, and an oil-filled liver, a shark is well buoyed up in the water. Sharks have a very keen sense of smell and can detect one drop of blood in a swimming pool full of water. Special jelly-filled pores on the shark's snout enable it to locate prey by sensing their electrical fields.

Marine mammal

Although they look like fish, whales are mammals. They have lungs and must come to the surface regularly to breathe air. Even a large whale has a thin skeleton because the water supports its body. If a whale became stranded on the shore, the unsupported weight of its body could crush its internal organs and it would be unlikely to survive.

Breathing underwater

This axolotl is a salamander that lives in Lake Xochimilico in Mexico. Like many water-living animals, it absorbs oxygen from the water through its pink, feathery gills. Gills fold outwards. If they folded inwards, like our lungs, they would quickly become clogged with stagnant water.

Still waters

Ponds and lakes are like giant puddles, with lakes larger than ponds. Most are fed by fresh water that runs off the surrounding land, or flows into them from rivers. Ponds and lakes are unique, because they contain water that is still rather than flowing. Lakes usually exist for hundreds or thousands of years. This seems like a long time to us, but compared to oceans and most rivers, lakes are short lived. Over the years, particles of sediment start to settle in a lake, eventually filling it so it dries out.

Tree pool
In rainforests, pools containing only a small amount of water often form where bromeliad plants grow on the trunks and branches of trees. These pools teem with all kinds of life, from plant and animal plankton to predators as large as frogs.

Wetlands
Swamps and other areas where the soil is waterlogged are known as wetlands. These areas are crucial water stores that supply water to rivers. Plants and microbes remove harmful substances from the water as it passes through the wetlands.

Important lakes

Baikal	Constance	Superior	Titicaca
This Russian lake is the deepest in the world and the largest lake by volume.	Lying between Switzerland, Germany, and Austria, Lake Constance supplies water to 4.5 million people.	The largest of the five North American Great Lakes, Superior is also the world's largest lake by area.	At an altitude of 3,812 m (12,516 ft), Titicaca is the highest big lake in the world.

Seasonal pool
Vernal pools fill with water in the wet season and turn to parched ground in the dry. When the rains return, dormant eggs hatch out and young (larvae) change form. The pond is soon bursting with brine shrimp and tadpole shrimp.

Invaded by reeds
When a lake starts to fill with sediment, reeds grow around its edges and the area of open water shrinks. Eventually, land plants grow where there were once reeds, and what was once a lake becomes an area of land.

Giant lakes
The biggest lakes are like inland seas. At 25 million years old, Lake Baikal in Russia is the world's most ancient lake. Unusually, it has not silted up because ground movement is causing its bedrock to sink as fast as sediment is added.

Victoria
The world's second largest lake by area is Lake Victoria in Africa.

Rivers

Most rivers begin life as a tiny stream running down a mountain slope. They are fed by melting snow and ice, or by rainwater running off the land. The water follows cracks and folds in the rock as it flows downhill. Streams meet and join together, growing larger and larger until the flow can be called a river. When the river reaches lower ground, it usually slows, widens, and takes a winding route. Eventually, most rivers empty into the sea.

Waterfall
Fast-flowing water in a river's upper reaches can carve out waterfalls. If the riverbed changes abruptly from hard to soft rock, the river erodes the softer rock. This leaves a steep cliff of hard rock, which becomes a waterfall.

V-shaped valley
High in the mountains, the river is narrow and fast flowing. Its water carries pebbles and boulders that erode the sides and bottom of the riverbed, cutting a V-shaped valley.

Meltwater
A stream fed by melted ice, or meltwater, shrinks and expands with the seasons. The stream gushes over its rocky bed in spring, but in winter may be reduced to just a trickle.

Rapids
If a river flows over a bed of varied rocks, the softer rocks are worn away, leaving hard rocks poking up through the water. The water swirls around these obstacles, creating rapids.

The rivers featured

Indus
Fed by snow in the Himalayas, the Indus eventually flows into the Arabian Sea.

Swift
This meltwater-fed river in Alaska, USA, shifts its course through the mountains from year to year.

Victoria Falls
These 108-m- (355-ft-) high falls on the Zambezi are known as "Mosi-oa-tunya", the smoke that thunders.

Mekong
Along the border of Thailand and Laos, the Mekong flows though spectacular rapids.

World's longest rivers

Nile (Africa) 6,700 km (4,160 miles) It has two major tributaries (branches) – the Blue Nile and the White Nile.

Amazon (South America) 6,430 km (3,990 miles) More water flows through the Amazon than any other river.

Yangtze (Asia) 5,500 km (3,420 miles) Reaching depths of more than 150 m (500 ft), the Yangtze is the world's deepest river.

Huang He (Asia) 5,460 km (3,390 miles) Also known as the Yellow River, this is the world's muddiest river.

Lena (Asia) 4,400 km (2,730 miles) Its lower course freezes for several months each winter.

Congo (Africa) 4,340 km (2,695 miles) The second largest river by volume of flow.

Meander
In its middle and lower reaches, a river flows in winding curves called meanders. Sometimes the river finds a shorter course by cutting across the land separating two parts of a meander. This leaves an abandoned lake, called an ox-bow lake, next to the river.

Floodplain
The land along a river's lower course is almost flat, slowing the river to a lazy pace. As the river nears its mouth, the river valley may become a wide plain, covered by sediment left behind when the river floods.

Delta
At its mouth, the river deposits some of the sand, silt, and clay it is carrying. This creates a wide platform, called a delta, which may split the river into several channels. Most deltas are roughly fan-shaped.

Mature river
In the middle of a river's course, the land slopes more gently, and the river broadens and flows more slowly. The water is often murky from the sediment it contains.

Thames
This UK river receives cleaned wastewater from more than 10 million people.

Amazon
In parts of its middle course, the Amazon is already more than 16 km (10 miles) wide.

Mara
This east African river meanders through savannah, a mix of tropical grasslands and trees.

Mississippi
The delta of the Mississippi river in the USA is shaped like a bird's foot.

Oceans

The oceans are unimaginably vast. Together, they make up more than 95 per cent of Earth's living space. The deepest parts of the ocean descend to more than 10 km (about 6 miles) and the cold, dark, high-pressure environment at the bottom is very different from the conditions at the surface. Fish and other marine animals have evolved body shapes and hunting techniques that enable them to survive at a particular level.

Coral reefs

These rocky structures grow in warm, clear, unpolluted shallow water. They are built by coral polyps – miniature animals that are related to sea anemones and jellyfish. About one-third of the ocean's animal and plant species lives among the nooks and crannies of coral reefs.

Sunlit zone

The sunlit zone lies in the upper 200 m (650 ft) of the sea where there is sufficient light for marine plants to photosynthesize (make food using light energy). The sunlit zone contains most of the sea's creatures that are familiar to us.

Twilight zone

At depths between 200 m (650 ft) and 1,000 m (3,300 ft) only sparse sunlight penetrates. In this twilight world some creatures make their own light (bioluminescence) to attract prey, confuse predators, or to identify each other. Many creatures rise closer to the surface at night to feed on plankton (drifting organisms).

Marine turtle
The eight species of marine turtle are air-breathing reptiles. Their varied diet includes jellyfish. Females dig nests on sandy beaches in which to lay their eggs.

Jellyfish
These are invertebrates (animals without backbones). Most swim sluggishly in the surface waters. They use stinging tentacles to capture smaller animals.

Sperm whale
This whale, an air-breathing mammal, can reach up to 18 m (60 ft) long. Some adults make amazingly deep dives into the twilight and dark zones in search of squid.

Marlin
The marlin hunts fish at high speed using its sword-like upper jaw to swipe and disable prey. It is the world's fastest fish with speeds of more than 110 km/h (68 mph).

Viperfish
This fish has a large mouth armed with long curved fangs. A viperfish wiggles a spine on its dorsal fin to attract prey close to its fiercesome mouth.

Lanternfish
Large eyes help lanternfish to locate animal plankton prey. The light-emitting patches on the head, flanks, and underside help them to recognize other members of their species.

Scuba diver can go down to depths of up to 282 m (925 ft).

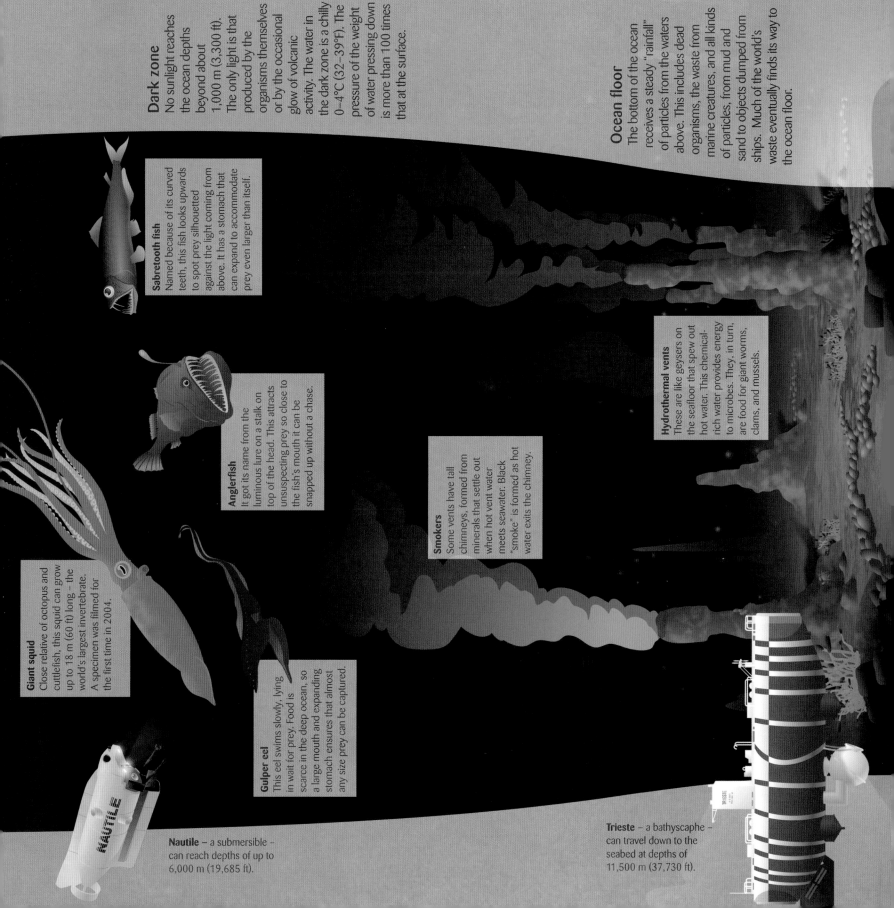

Dark zone

No sunlight reaches the ocean depths beyond about 1,000 m (3,300 ft). The only light is that produced by the organisms themselves or by the occasional glow of volcanic activity. The water in the dark zone is a chilly 0–4°C (32–39°F). The pressure of the weight of water pressing down is more than 100 times that at the surface.

Ocean floor

The bottom of the ocean receives a steady "rainfall" of particles from the waters above. This includes dead organisms, the waste from marine creatures, and all kinds of particles, from mud and sand to objects dumped from ships. Much of the world's waste eventually finds its way to the ocean floor.

Sabretooth fish
Named because of its curved teeth, this fish looks upwards to spot prey silhouetted against the light coming from above. It has a stomach that can expand to accommodate prey even larger than itself.

Anglerfish
It got its name from the luminous lure on a stalk on top of the head. This attracts unsuspecting prey so close to the fish's mouth it can be snapped up without a chase.

Giant squid
Close relative of octopus and cuttlefish, this squid can grow up to 18 m (60 ft) long – the world's largest invertebrate. A specimen was filmed for the first time in 2004.

Gulper eel
This eel swims slowly, lying in wait for prey. Food is scarce in the deep ocean, so a large mouth and expanding stomach ensures that almost any size prey can be captured.

Smokers
Some vents have tall chimneys, formed from minerals that settle out when hot vent water meets seawater. Black "smoke" is formed as hot water exits the chimney.

Hydrothermal vents
These are like geysers on the seafloor that spew out hot water. This chemical-rich water provides energy to microbes. They, in turn, are food for giant worms, clams, and mussels.

Nautile – a submersible – can reach depths of up to 6,000 m (19,685 ft).

Trieste – a bathyscaphe – can travel down to the seabed at depths of 11,500 m (37,730 ft).

Tides and currents

Gravitational attraction
Like all large, dense objects in space, the Moon pulls other objects towards it. This is called its gravitational attraction. As the Moon orbits the Earth, it pulls the water on Earth's surface towards it. This creates a bulge of water travelling around the Earth.

The water in the oceans is constantly on the move. The pull of the Moon drags water across the Earth's surface, producing surges called tides. Winds blowing across Earth's surface stir and steer seawater, creating flows of water called currents, and whipping up its surface to make waves. And the Earth spinning on its axis turns the surges and currents, a feature called the Coriolis effect.

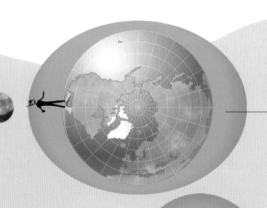

High tide occurs where seawater bulges due to the pull of the Moon.

Low tide occurs where water has been pulled away into the bulge.

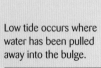

Tidal bulge
The Moon's pull causes the ocean tides. Water that is closest to the Moon is pulled outwards, creating a bulge. A similar bulge appears on the opposite side of the Earth as here the water is furthest away and only weakly attracted. Where the bulge lies it is high tide, and in places where water has been withdrawn it is low tide. Most coastal areas have two high tides and two low tides each day as the Earth turns.

High tide
The Bay of Fundy in Canada funnels water to a narrow point where the world's largest tides occur. During the biggest tides of the year, the difference in level between high water (shown here) and low water can be an astonishing 17 m (56 ft).

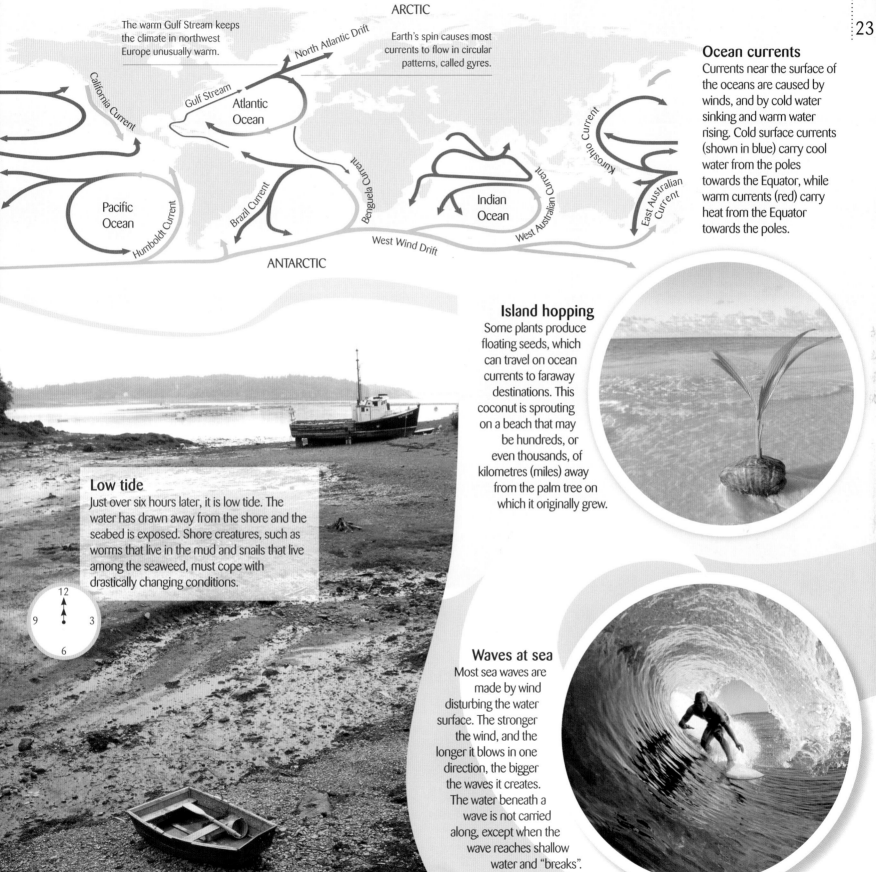

ARCTIC

23

The warm Gulf Stream keeps the climate in northwest Europe unusually warm.

Earth's spin causes most currents to flow in circular patterns, called gyres.

North Atlantic Drift

California Current

Gulf Stream

Atlantic Ocean

Kuroshio Current

Pacific Ocean

Humboldt Current

Brazil Current

Benguela Current

Indian Ocean

West Australian Current

East Australian Current

West Wind Drift

ANTARCTIC

Ocean currents

Currents near the surface of the oceans are caused by winds, and by cold water sinking and warm water rising. Cold surface currents (shown in blue) carry cool water from the poles towards the Equator, while warm currents (red) carry heat from the Equator towards the poles.

Island hopping

Some plants produce floating seeds, which can travel on ocean currents to faraway destinations. This coconut is sprouting on a beach that may be hundreds, or even thousands, of kilometres (miles) away from the palm tree on which it originally grew.

Low tide

Just over six hours later, it is low tide. The water has drawn away from the shore and the seabed is exposed. Shore creatures, such as worms that live in the mud and snails that live among the seaweed, must cope with drastically changing conditions.

Waves at sea

Most sea waves are made by wind disturbing the water surface. The stronger the wind, and the longer it blows in one direction, the bigger the waves it creates. The water beneath a wave is not carried along, except when the wave reaches shallow water and "breaks".

Shaping the land

Water is one of the most powerful forces scraping and shaping the Earth's surface. Whether in its liquid form or as ice, water carves out valleys, wears away coastlines, and carries particles of rock down rivers and across oceans. If water breaks rock down into particles where it stands, the process is called weathering. If water wears rock away and carries its particles from one place to another, the process is known as erosion.

Cut by a river
In northern Arizona, USA, layers of sediment, deposited on the bottom of ancient seas, have been raised onto land by great forces underground. In the last few million years, the mighty Colorado River has cut a 1.6-km (1-mile) deep valley, the Grand Canyon, through this plateau.

Coastal erosion
When a storm wave crashes against a rocky shore its force can be as strong as the thrust of the space shuttle's main engines. Over the years, the waves erode the edge of the land, opening up cracks, dislodging chunks of rock, and often creating a natural arch.

Pillars of weathered rock
These strangely shaped pillars are known as hoodoos. Made of soft limestone rock, capped by harder rock, they are shaped by frost and rain. In winter, frost and ice crack the rocks. In warmer weather, rainwater, which is slightly acidic, slowly dissolves the limestone and rounds the hoodoo's edges to create this shape.

Rivers of snow and ice
When snow and ice settle on high ground, gravity gradually pulls them down along any valleys. This forms a flowing "river" of ice, called a glacier. The moving ice enters cracks in the rock, dislodges rocky chunks, and wears away the bottom and sides of the valley.

Ice and frost
Rainwater or melting snow seep into cracks in any exposed rock. If this water freezes, it expands and creates wedges of ice. These can cause enormous damage, prising any cracks wider and splitting the rock.

Biological weathering
Plants contain lots of water. As they grow, their expanding roots and branches have the power to crack open and dislodge rock. This disused temple in Cambodia is gradually being ripped apart by invading trees.

Chemical weathering
This limestone carving of a bird on a French church has been worn away by centuries of rainfall. The acid in rainwater has dissolved the stone. In recent years, sulphur dioxide from power station emissions and other air pollutants have made rain much more acidic.

Glacier facts	Ice age	Glacier speed	Glacier depth	Glacier loss
	About 18,000 years ago, at the height of the last ice age, almost a third of all land was covered by snow and ice.	A typical glacier creeps along even more slowly than a snail. It advances only about 10 m (33 ft) in a year.	Ice in a glacier can be 3,000 m (10,000 ft) deep. It may hide a maze of meltwater streams that carve through the ice.	At one time, there were 150 glaciers in Glacier National Park in the USA, but now only 27 remain.

Air moves in giant circuits, called cells. There are three cells in each hemisphere. This is the north polar cell.

Weather

This cell lies over the mid-latitude region. It carries warm air north over southern Europe.

In this tropical cell, warm air is rising near the Equator, then flowing north.

On a hot summer day or a wet winter night, when there are high winds or snow storms, it is always the relationship between air, water, and heat that is responsible. Ever-changing quantities of these three elements produce the wide variety of weather systems experienced around the world. Our weather occurs in the lowest part of the atmosphere, which extends about 12 km (7 miles) above Earth.

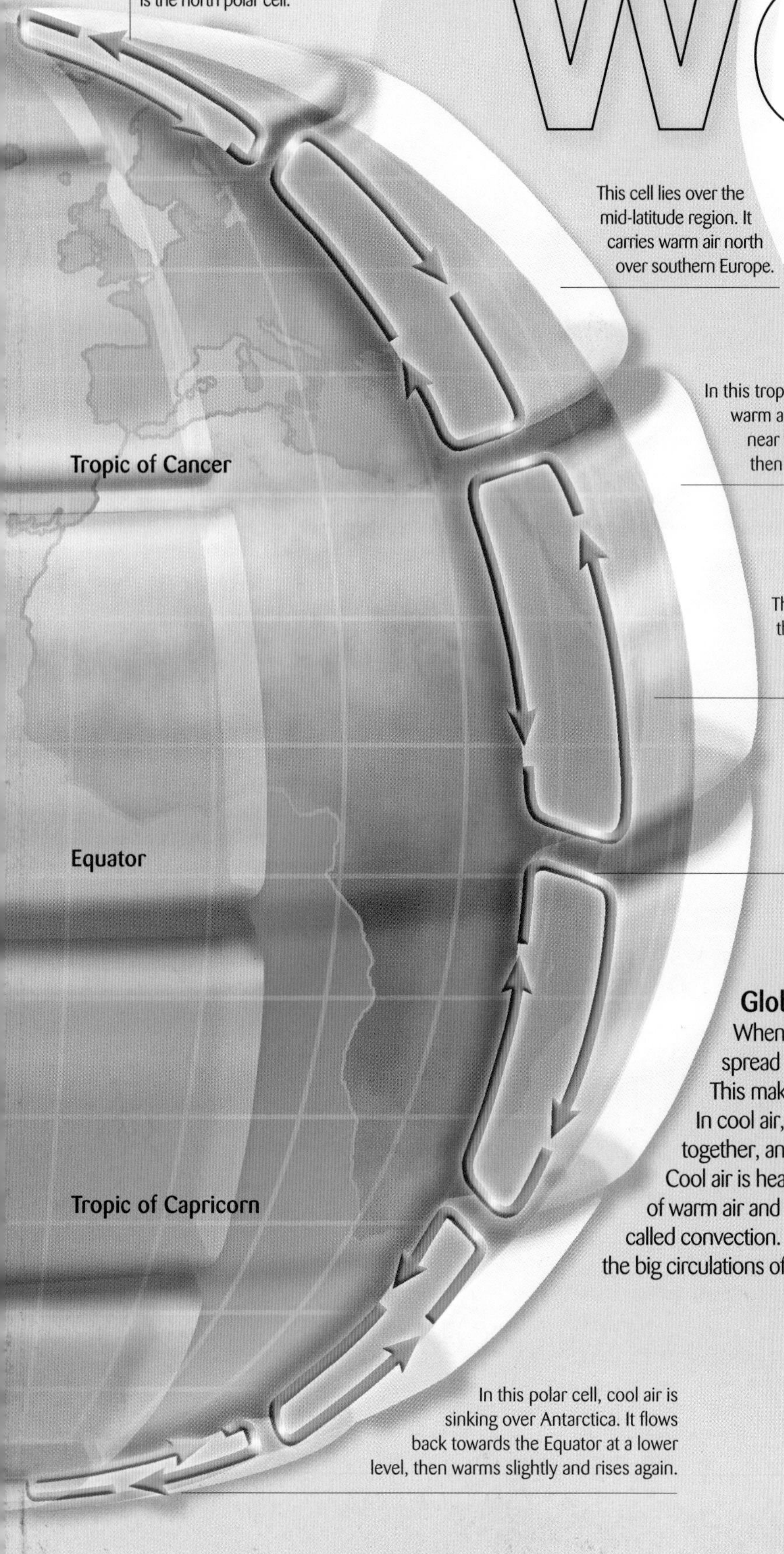

Tropic of Cancer

The cells distribute heat over the globe. Overall, they carry cold air away from the poles and warm air towards them.

Warm, moist air (shown red) rises, then starts to cool down. Cool air (shown blue) warms up as it sinks towards the ground.

Equator

Global air circulation
When air warms up, its gas molecules spread out and occupy more space. This makes warm air lighter, so it rises. In cool air, the molecules huddle closer together, and take up less space. Cool air is heavier, so it sinks. The rising of warm air and sinking of cool air is called convection. It helps to generate the big circulations of air across the globe.

Tropic of Capricorn

In this polar cell, cool air is sinking over Antarctica. It flows back towards the Equator at a lower level, then warms slightly and rises again.

Weather patterns
Climate is the pattern of weather in a particular area over many years. At the Equator, the weather is always warm and often wet. Near the poles, conditions are cold and often dry. In between, weather conditions vary. But whatever the climate, it shapes the lives of local plants and animals. The African savannah, shown here, has a hot climate where rainfall is highly seasonal.

Frontal systems

An air mass is a large chunk of air in the lower atmosphere. It could be warm or cold, and wet or dry. An air mass is largely responsible for the weather on the ground below it. Where two air masses meet, at places called fronts, they bring changeable weather. If cold air flows under warm air, it creates a cold front, and it produces violent weather. Warm air flowing over cold air creates a warm front, and brings steady rain.

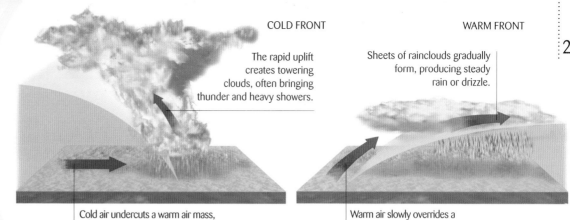

COLD FRONT

The rapid uplift creates towering clouds, often bringing thunder and heavy showers.

Cold air undercuts a warm air mass, forcing it to rise sharply.

WARM FRONT

Sheets of rainclouds gradually form, producing steady rain or drizzle.

Warm air slowly overrides a cold air mass.

A steady downpour

Raindrops form when water vapour in rising air changes from a gas to a liquid (condenses). This forms tiny water droplets, which gradually join together to make raindrops. The uplift that makes air rise and create rain clouds can occur where water or moist land warms up, where winds collide, at fronts, or where moving air is forced upwards to pass over higher ground. A downpour can unload 2–5 cm (0.8–2 in) of rain in a single hour.

Hailstones

Pellets of ice that fall from clouds are called hailstones. They form when ice crystals rise and fall repeatedly inside storm clouds. The hailstones gradually accumulate more and more ice, growing larger until they are heavy enough to fall from the sky. In some places, hailstones the size of tennis balls can fall.

Wild weather

Hurricanes form above warm tropical seas, where water is evaporating rapidly from the sea surface. The water condenses higher in the atmosphere, releasing heat. This creates great instability, with winds blowing at more than 119 km/h (74 mph) and storm clouds that drop torrential rain. In 2005, Hurricane Katrina forced millions of people to evacuate the southeastern USA, and killed at least 1,300 people.

Nimbostratus

Clouds are named after their shape, their height in the atmosphere (altitude), and other key features. In Latin, nimbus means "rain" and stratus means "layered", so these are flat, layered rainclouds. Usually dark in colour, nimbostratus clouds cause prolonged heavy rain.

Cumulus

If the sky is full of giant puffs of cotton wool, cumulus clouds have gathered. Meaning "heap" in Latin, cumulus clouds are seen mostly on sunny days. They form by the process of convection – the land warms air that rises as "thermals", which cool to form the cloud.

Clouds

It is unusual to look up into a cloudless sky. Most of the time, there are clouds floating high above us. They are the result of moisture in the air condensing to form minute water droplets or ice crystals. These droplets or crystals are so tiny that they stay suspended in the air. But when groups of droplets or crystals combine, they become heavier. At this point, water droplets fall to the ground as rain, while ice crystals fall as snow or hail.

Cloud formation

A cumulus cloud starts life as a pocket of especially warm, moist air. Being warmer than the surrounding air, it is also lighter, so it starts to rise, like a helium balloon. This rising air, called a thermal, expands and cools as it gets higher. When its temperature reaches the dew point, it starts to condense into liquid water droplets, which form the cloud.

Air cooled to temperature of surroundings, so no longer rises. This is the top of the cloud. — 3,000 m (10,000 ft)

Air has cooled to dew point. Water condenses to form cloud droplets. — 2,000 m (6,500 ft)

Air rises as swirling bubble, expanding and cooling. — 1,000 m (3,300 ft)

A pocket of warm air breaks away from the ground and rises because it is lighter than the surrounding, cooler air. — 0

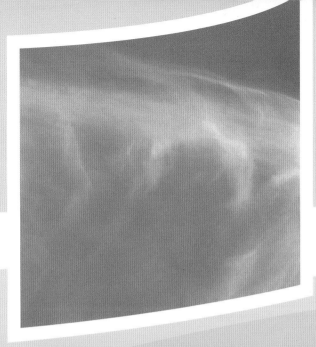

Altostratus
These clouds form a mid-height grey layer higher than cumulus, but below cirrus, and can often cover vast sections of sky. Altostratus is made up of a mixture of ice and water. When the layer is thin, a ghostly Sun shines through.

Cirrus
These feathery, white clouds are aptly named cirrus – the Latin for "wisp of hair". Made up of ice crystals, cirrus clouds streak the sky at high altitude. A type of cirrus, called cirrus uncinus, are known as mares' tails because the clouds resemble horses' tails.

Cumulonimbus
A thunderstorm is brewing when fully developed cumulonimbus clouds gather in the sky. These giant versions of cumulus clouds can be 8 km (5 miles) in height. The biggest cumulonimbus clouds can create hurricanes and tornadoes in warmer parts of the world.

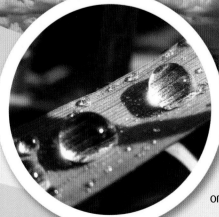

Dew point
The temperature at which water vapour in the air begins to condense and form droplets is called the dew point. If water vapour condenses directly onto the ground, it forms dew.

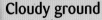

Cloudy ground
Mist and fog are simply clouds that form at ground level. Fog is thicker than mist because it contains more water droplets. If visibility is less than 1 km (0.6 miles), it is classed as fog. As the sun comes up, fog usually clears.

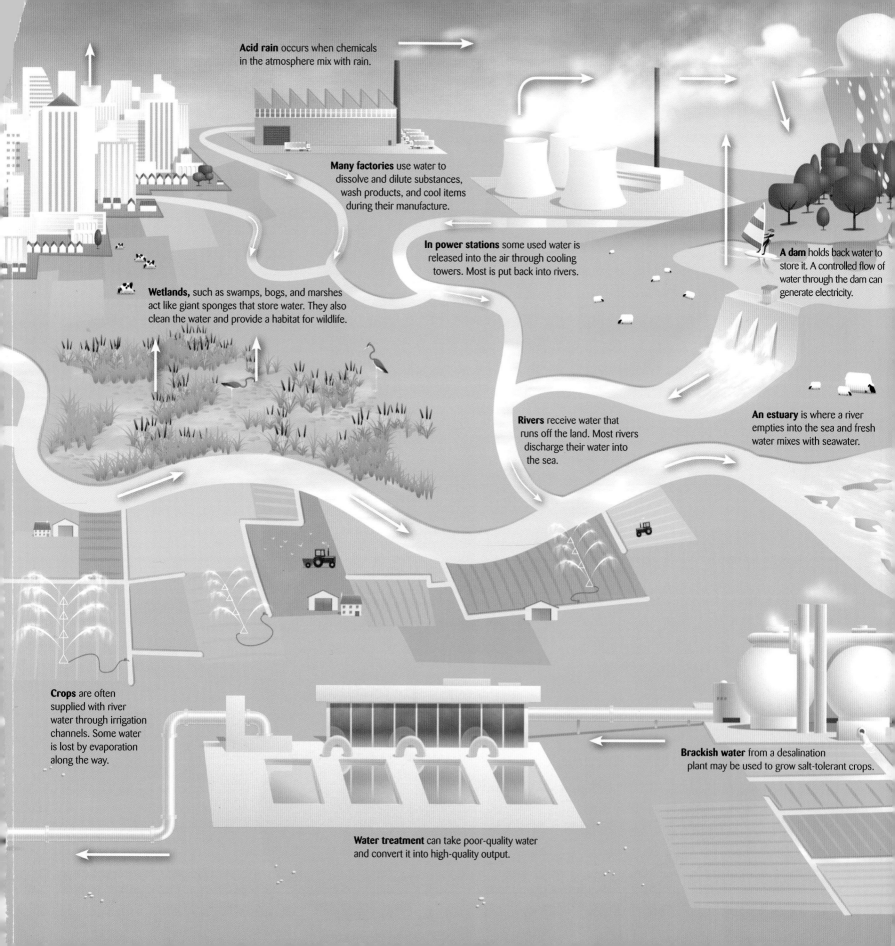

Acid rain occurs when chemicals in the atmosphere mix with rain.

Many factories use water to dissolve and dilute substances, wash products, and cool items during their manufacture.

In power stations some used water is released into the air through cooling towers. Most is put back into rivers.

A dam holds back water to store it. A controlled flow of water through the dam can generate electricity.

Wetlands, such as swamps, bogs, and marshes act like giant sponges that store water. They also clean the water and provide a habitat for wildlife.

Rivers receive water that runs off the land. Most rivers discharge their water into the sea.

An estuary is where a river empties into the sea and fresh water mixes with seawater.

Crops are often supplied with river water through irrigation channels. Some water is lost by evaporation along the way.

Water treatment can take poor-quality water and convert it into high-quality output.

Brackish water from a desalination plant may be used to grow salt-tolerant crops.

On the move

On Earth, there is a finite supply of water. It constantly moves around the planet in mini water cycles that may take hours or thousands of years to complete. It travels through pipes, rivers, oceans, forests, deserts, rocks, animals, people, the food we eat, and the air that we breathe. It is even possible that ocean currents still carry tiny amounts of Julius Caesar's bathwater. This artwork shows the many ways water moves around an imaginary landscape.

In cities moist air gushes from office air-conditioning systems and steam belches from car exhausts.

In towns water evaporates from all wet surfaces including roofs and gardens. Steam enters the air through chimneys.

Waste from toilets is known as foul waste and is removed from homes via pipes to a sewage plant for treatment.

Sewage plant treats waste water from homes and businesses to make it safe to release into a river.

Washing line evaporation is greatest on hot, dry, windy days. This is when water from damp clothes evaporates the fastest.

A hot shower uses about 15 litres (4 gal) of water per minute. The used water goes down the drain and into a wastewater pipe.

A car wash uses at least 120 litres (32 gal) of water per car. The used water goes down the drain and soon reaches a sewer.

Underground reservoir stores water before it is distributed to homes and businesses.

Water cycle

Condensation

Precipitation

Evaporation

Precipitation

is the word used to describe the different forms of water that fall or settle from the sky. This includes rain, snow, sleet (icy rain), hail (ice pellets), frost, and dew. Precipitation is how water in the air returns to Earth's surface.

Percolation

Percolation

is the movement of water through soil and rocks as ground water. It begins with infiltration – water soaking into the ground. Water can take from hours to thousands of years to gather in water-supplying layers of rock underground, called aquifers.

Groundwater flow

The world's water circulates between sea, air, and land. As it moves, it often changes from one state – solid, liquid, or gas – to another. The water cycle is powered by the Sun's heat, which evaporates water from sea and land. Some of the moisture in the air then condenses into water droplets or freezes into ice particles, which may fall as precipitation. Water gathers in rivers and lakes, and percolates through rock and soil, eventually moving downhill to the sea.

Condensation
is the process of a gas turning to a liquid, as seen in the dew on this spider's web. When air becomes cold, its water vapour separates out as droplets, which can form clouds. When the droplets in clouds merge, they can become raindrops, large enough to fall out of the sky.

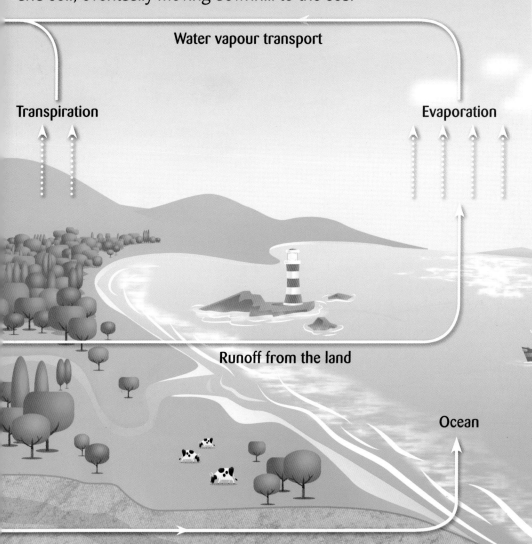

Water vapour transport

Transpiration

Evaporation

Runoff from the land

Ocean

Evaporation
occurs when molecules of a liquid break free and become gas (steam). Water evaporates all the time from the sea, lakes, rivers, and wet surfaces on land, such as a roof. This adds moisture to the air, which travels around the planet on winds and eventually falls as precipitation.

Transpiration
is the evaporation of water from plants. By channelling water through their extensive system of roots and leaves, plants make the evaporation process faster than evaporation directly from the soil. Dense tropical forests release so much water vapour that they become cloaked in mist.

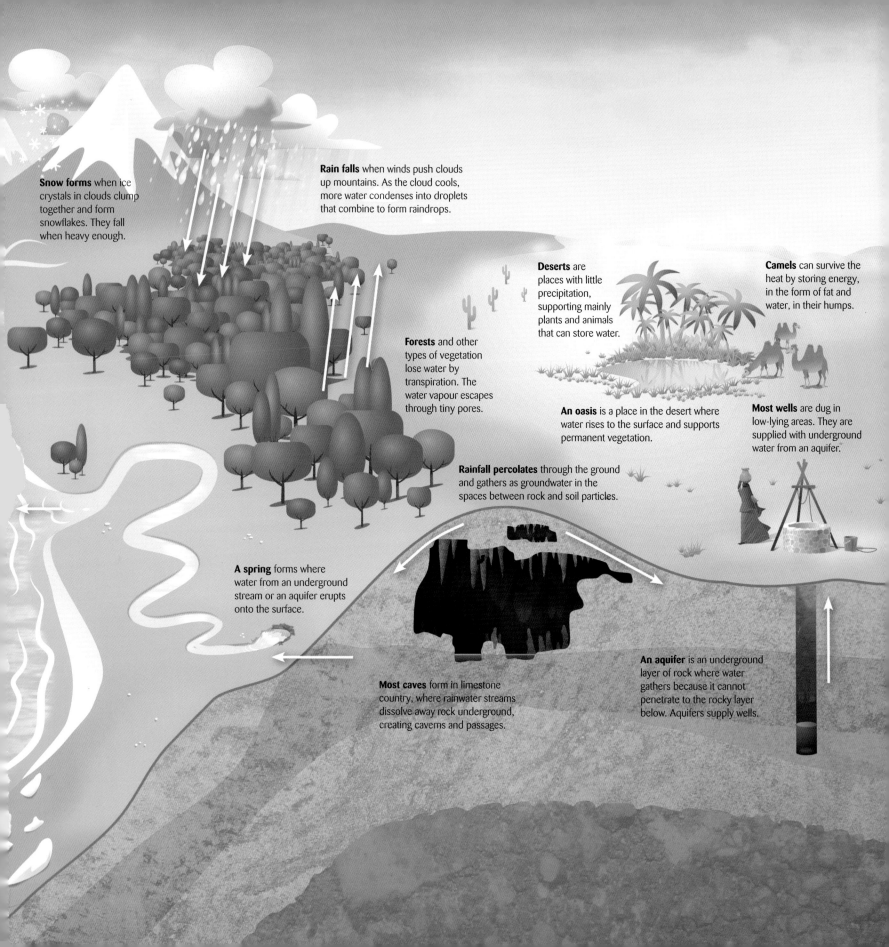

Snow forms when ice crystals in clouds clump together and form snowflakes. They fall when heavy enough.

Rain falls when winds push clouds up mountains. As the cloud cools, more water condenses into droplets that combine to form raindrops.

Deserts are places with little precipitation, supporting mainly plants and animals that can store water.

Camels can survive the heat by storing energy, in the form of fat and water, in their humps.

Forests and other types of vegetation lose water by transpiration. The water vapour escapes through tiny pores.

An oasis is a place in the desert where water rises to the surface and supports permanent vegetation.

Most wells are dug in low-lying areas. They are supplied with underground water from an aquifer.

Rainfall percolates through the ground and gathers as groundwater in the spaces between rock and soil particles.

A spring forms where water from an underground stream or an aquifer erupts onto the surface.

Most caves form in limestone country, where rainwater streams dissolve away rock underground, creating caverns and passages.

An aquifer is an underground layer of rock where water gathers because it cannot penetrate to the rocky layer below. Aquifers supply wells.

The Sun's heat powers the water cycle by evaporating water and making it rise by means of convection.

Aircraft flying at high altitudes can pick up frost on their wings. They may carry this vast distances before it melts.

Clouds may form as air rises and its moisture condenses into water droplets or freezes into ice crystals.

Water evaporating from the sea accounts for about 80 per cent of total evaporation.

Meltwater from thawing ice and snow in the mountains feeds many of the world's largest rivers.

Hurricanes develop in the tropics above warm seas. These giant storms cycle millions of tonnes of water each day.

Breath of a blue whale contains several litres (gal) of water. All air-breathing animals lose water into the air through their breath.

The oceans hold 9[...] of the world's sur[...] Their heat and m[...] transferred to t[...] the world's we[...]

Desalination plant removes salt from seawater, allowing the water to be used for irrigation or even for drinking.

The iceberg that sank the "Titanic" came from a Greenland ice sheet, where it had lain for thousands of years. The collision released water vapour into the air.

Glaciers on land, [...] iceberg [...] most o[...] fresh [...]

Body water

Water is essential to human life – it makes up more than half your body weight, is the main component of each of your 100 billion body cells, and without it, you would die in just a few days. The amount of water inside your body must remain almost constant for good health. Losing even 10 per cent of your body weight in water is enough to make you seriously ill. The amount of water leaving your body through sweating and weeing must be replaced by regular drinking and eating. If the body's water content drops, a part of the brain called the hypothalamus detects the change and triggers the thirst response.

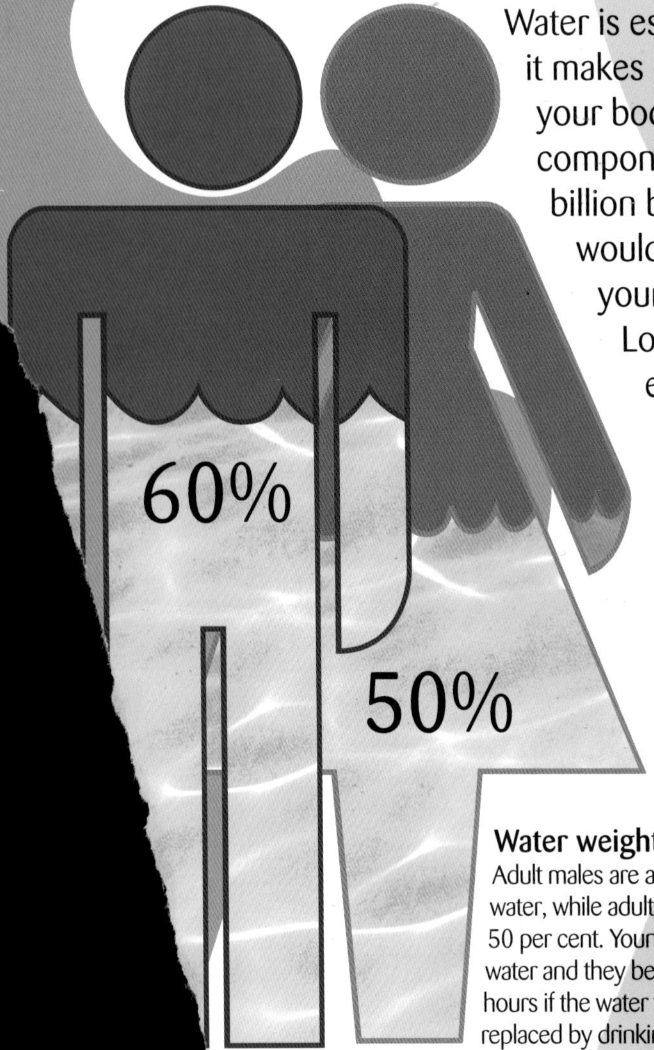

60%

50%

Water weight
Adult males are at least 60 per cent water, while adult females are at least 50 per cent. Young babies are 70 per cent water and they become ill within a few hours if the water they lose is not replaced by drinking milk.

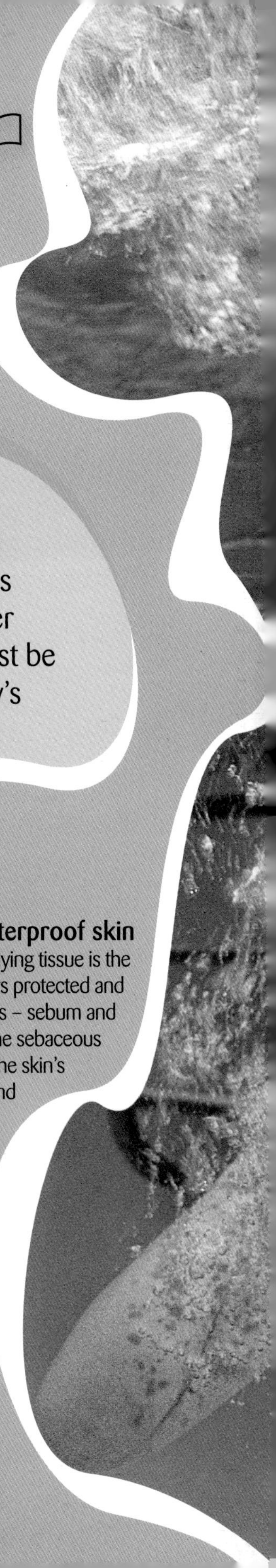

Waterproof skin
The skin and its underlying tissue is the largest organ in the body. It stays protected and waterproof thanks to two substances – sebum and keratin. Produced under the skin in the sebaceous glands, sebum is a natural oil that keeps the skin's outer layer, the epidermis, lubricated and water-repellent. Also present is the tough protein keratin, which acts as a barrier, preventing liquid from entering the skin.

Muscle	Fat	Bone
75%	25%	22%

Blood army

The blood flowing through your body consists of red and white blood cells suspended in a liquid called plasma, which is 90 per cent water. As well as transporting oxygen, food, and wastes, blood is also responsible for fighting disease and sealing damaged skin.

Digestive juices

During a meal, these "pits" in the stomach lining pour 0.5 litres (0.9 pt) of juice onto your food. This juice contains digestive enzymes that break down food. Deep in the intestines, digestive juices further break down food. Almost all the water found in these juices is recovered in the large intestine.

Flexible joints

The freedom to move easily comes from joints in the skeleton and the muscles used to bend them. Bones would grind together and wear away at the joint without watery synovial fluid. This is secreted by a membrane to lubricate joints. The gaps on this X-ray of a knee joint are full of synovial fluid.

Working up a sweat

Water leaves the body in four ways. About 1.5 litres (2.6 pt) of water a day exit the body in the form of urine, 0.4 litre (0.7 pt) gets breathed out, and about 0.1 litre (0.2 pt) is lost in solid waste, or faeces. A further 0.5 litre (0.9 pt) of water escapes through the skin as sweat. By evaporating on the skin, sweat helps to cool us down. Exercise, stress, and heat often increase sweat production.

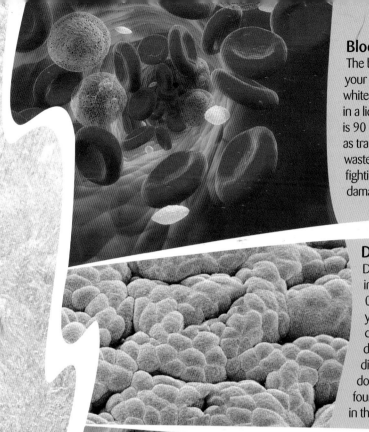

Water power

Water is heavy, there are vast amounts of it on Earth's surface, and it can move with considerable force. It has the power to do work, making it an excellent source of energy. People use dams to capture a river's kinetic energy (energy of movement) and potential energy (such as energy released by a change in height). Hydroelectric dams convert water's energy into electrical power to supply homes, offices, and industry.

Hydroelectric power

The Grand Coulee dam on the Colorado River, USA is a barrier built across a valley to trap and temporarily store the moving water in a river. As in other hydroelectric dams, water flows through tunnels or tubes in the dam, turning propeller-like structures called turbines. These generate electricity.

Power of the tides

In some places, the tides can be harnessed to generate electricity. This requires a big tidal surge, with a difference between water levels at high and low tide of 7.5 m (25 ft) or more. Modern tidal barrages work in a similar way to hydroelectric dams. Some are two-directional, generating power from both the rising and the falling tide. The Rance Tidal Barrage in Brittany, northern France, operates in this way and supplies electricity to more than 150,000 homes.

Falkirk Wheel

Scotland's Falkirk Wheel is cleverly designed to raise or lower barges to a height of 24 m (79 ft) using very little energy. When a barge enters one of the wheel's two containers, it pushes out an equal weight of water, so the overall weight of the container does not change. The two containers are counterbalanced, so as one rises, the other descends. Turning the wheel uses only the same amount of energy as boiling eight kettles of water.

Giant turbine

This is one of Grand Coulee's 33 turbines being fitted. When installed, water flows past the turbine blades, turning a shaft connected to an electricity generator. The huge pressure of the water stored in the reservoir behind the dam pushes water through the turbine blades at high speed.

Indian dam protest

Hydroelectric dams are a clean source of energy and cheap to run. However, they can have huge disadvantages. To build the reservoirs, it is necessary to flood large areas, often destroying people's homes. Changing the river's flow can also spread water-related diseases. These villagers in India are protesting because a proposed dam will flood their neighbourhood, forcing them to move.

Gushing geysers

Hot molten rock from deep under the ground can rise quite close to Earth's surface and warm the rainwater that gathers there. This causes steam and hot water to erupt at regular intervals through openings called geysers, as shown here in Yellowstone National Park, USA.

Welling up

In some places, people can dig or drill a well down to the water table and reach supplies of fresh water. Many wells are fed by aquifers – layers of underground rocks through which water moves easily. In most wells, water has to be pumped to the surface, but in an artesian well, water rises naturally under pressure.

Water table

Ground water rises to a level called the water table. Below this level, any spaces between the rock and soil particles are full of water, so the ground is saturated. The water table usually rises and falls with the seasons, getting higher during the wet season and lower during the dry season. The water surface of rivers and lakes usually lies level with the water table.

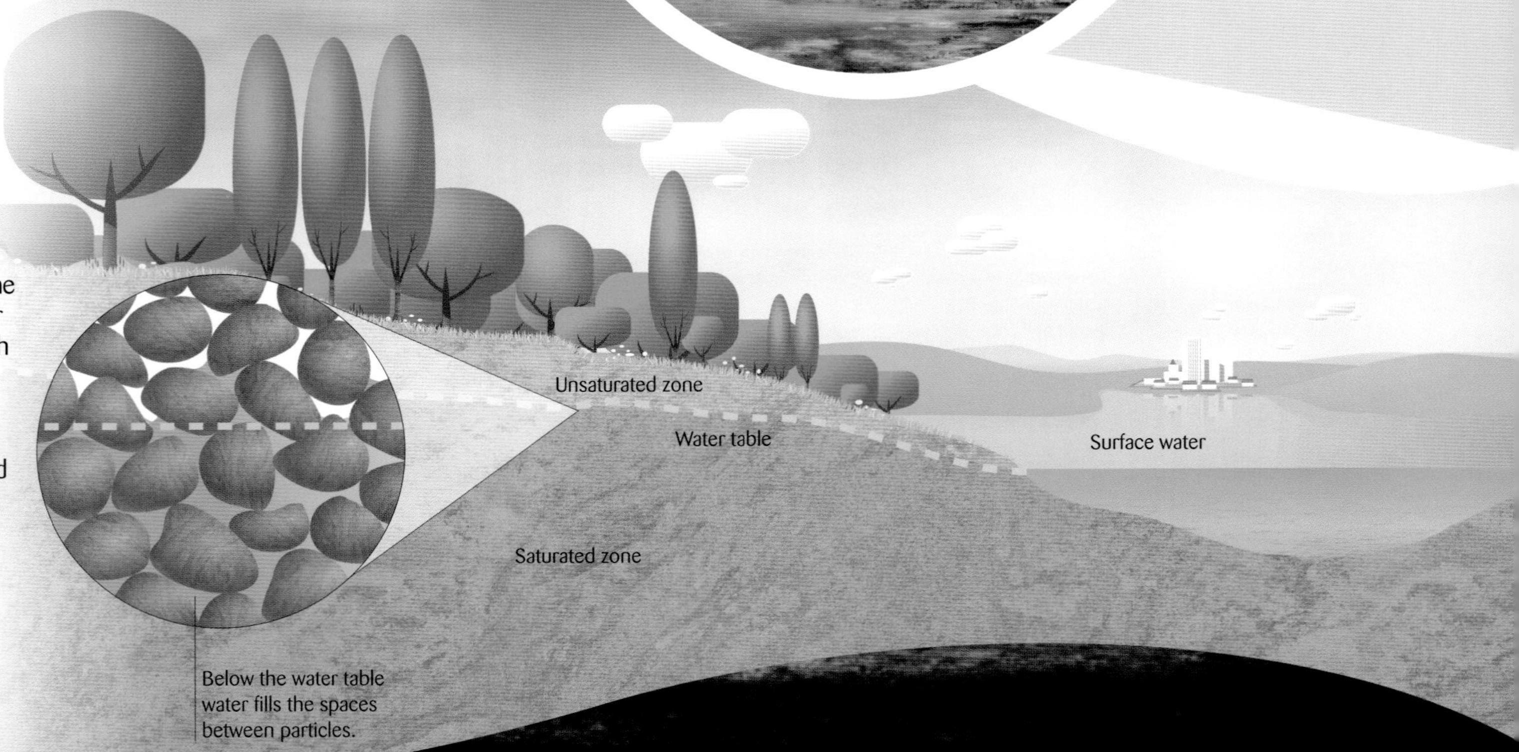

Surface water

Water table

Unsaturated zone

Saturated zone

Below the water table water fills the spaces between particles.

Underground

Beneath your feet lies one-quarter of Earth's fresh water. Any rain that does not run into lakes or rivers, or evaporate in the air, seeps underground into the soil and rock. This water travels down until it reaches a layer of rock that is too hard to soak through. Above this layer, the water collects, filling the cracks and spaces. Called ground water, it supplies the world's wells and springs.

Cave shapes

Most caves are carved from limestone rock by streams that flow underground. The streams carry rainwater, which is slightly acidic and dissolves the chemical calcium carbonate in limestone. Once a cave has formed, water rich in dissolved calcium carbonate may drip from its ceiling. This eventually deposits stalactites — icicle-shaped calcium carbonate hanging from the roof. Where drips splash onto the floor, candle-like stalagmites grow upwards.

Urban water

Within towns and cities around the world there is a constant demand for water. This is needed for a vast range of uses, such as flushing toilets, supplying car washes, and operating industrial machinery. The water that arrives in homes, offices, and factories needs to be of good quality. And, once used, the dirty water has to be disposed of safely. Under the ground, a network of pipes delivers water to and from the places where it is needed.

Water treatment

Sewage is another name for general waste water. It includes liquid waste from toilets, baths, and kitchens. Underground pipes carry this waste to a sewage works where contaminants are removed. In the treatment works, waste water is left to settle so that floating solids can be scraped from the surface and sinking solids removed. The water may be filtered and chemically treated before it is safe to return to the environment.

Safe to drink

Most tap water comes from a river, spring, or well. Domestic water is usually treated in a water supply facility before it is safe to use. The water arrives in your area through underground pipes called the mains supply.

Bad bacteria

Diseases such as cholera, typhoid, and polio can be caught by drinking water that contains harmful microbes. The microbes shown here (magnified) live naturally in the human gut. The form of this microbe from cows makes people ill if it gets into water.

Down the plughole

The water that empties down the sink runs to a main wastewater pipe that leaves the property. This, in turn, joins up with a larger pipe or underground channel called a sewer. Networks of sewers carry waste water, which flows downhill under gravity or is pushed along by pumps. Sewers receive all kinds of waste water, including water that runs off the streets and water from offices and factories.

Sewer robot

Sewer pipes often run deep underground. Workers enter sewers through vertical shafts to inspect them for damage or blockages. Intelligent robots, armed with lights and a video camera, make these inspections easier. Some robots are operated by remote control, but the control cables can get tangled round bends. The latest high-tech robots, such as this German version, only need a digital map of the sewers to get to any point and examine the pipes.

Emergency water

Fire hydrants are a crucial part of the emergency water systems. The water that supplies hydrants comes from large tanks usually located on hilltops. These tanks often connect to hydrants by a system of pipes laid out in a grid pattern. This allows water to travel from any tank to any hydrant via several routes. Firefighters, such as these in New York, attach a hose to a hydrant and open the valve with a wrench. Water then runs down from the tank, through the pipes, and blasts out of the hose at high pressure.

Greening the desert
It is possible to grow crops in deserts, as long as there is some rainfall or dew that can be harvested. Alternatively, water can be brought in from elsewhere. By growing plants close together, as here in Chile, it creates a region of moist air around the plants, which cuts down evaporation.

Microirrigation
When water is sprayed onto the land, a quarter of it may never reach the plant roots because it evaporates from the soil surface. Microirrigation is a system of piping water directly to the plants, with only as much water as needed trickling out. Here, onion plants are being irrigated in this way.

Rural water

Worldwide, more than 60 per cent of supplied water is used for agriculture – to feed crops and to provide drinking water and food plants for domestic animals. Irrigation, which controls the supply of water to farmland, can be an efficient way for farmers to use water. However, the demand for water from towns and cities, as well as for the land, almost exceeds supply, and people need to find ways to get "more crop from each drop".

Water for livestock
Livestock, such as these beef cattle, need plenty of water if they are to thrive. They drink water daily, and the grass and other plants they eat need water to grow. Extra cattle feed – such as pellets made from barley – need water to produce them too. If the cattle are brought into sheds, these must be washed down regularly. All in all, a single animal requires tens of litres of water a day to keep it healthy.

Rice paddy terrace

Farmers in southeast Asia make the best use of the land by cutting terraces into the sides of the hills. Rain fills these thin strips of land, which makes them ideal for growing rice. More than half the world's population relies on rice as a major part of their diet.

Greenhouse

Cultivating plants in a greenhouse is one way of conserving water while controlling the conditions under which they grow. Water that evaporates from the soil or transpires from the plants stays longer within a greenhouse. High-value crops, such as tomatoes, are often grown this way.

Sewage reed beds

Waste water from farms is usually rich in nutrients but may also contain waste matter and organisms from domestic animals. This water can be harmful to people and wildlife if emptied into the sea or a river. Beds planted with reeds, such as this one in Scotland, can naturally clean waste water. Bacteria (microbes) in the soil beneath the reeds digest the sewage and help to purify the water.

Water for food production

It is surprising how much water is used to produce food – and how widely that requirement varies. For plants, it takes almost twice as much water to grow rice than it does the equivalent weight of oranges. Animal produce, such as chicken and beef, requires even greater amounts. This is because domestic animals eat plants that have already been grown using water, and the animals then need their own supply of water as well. This chart compares how much water is needed to produce 1 kg (2.2 lb) of some popular foods.

oranges need 1,000 litres (1,760 pt)

wheat needs 1,200 litres (2,112 pt)

rice needs 2,000 litres (3,520 pt)

chicken needs 6,000 litres (10,558 pt)

beef needs 15,000 litres (26,396 pt)

Water and industry

From food to fabric, crayons to cars, and petrol to paper, virtually everything we use or consume needs water to make it. Water can be involved in chemical reactions, such as producing hydrogen or making plastics. In many cases, water acts as a solvent, dissolving and diluting chemicals. For the metal and electrics industries, water transfers heat, cools objects down, and cleans products. In some developed countries, more than half of the entire water supply is used by industries.

Cooling towers
In power stations, the process of burning fossil fuels releases heat. This turns large amounts of liquid water into steam, which drives turbines to generate electricity. Inside a power station's cooling towers, evaporation cools waste water so that it can be returned to the river from where it originally came.

Petrochemical works

Deep below the seabed and some parts of the ground lie petroleum oil and natural gas. These fossil fuels are drilled out for the petrochemical industry. They are used in the production of organic (carbon-containing) chemicals, involved in making plastics, paints, detergents, and other household items. Water plays an essential part – 10 litres (18 pt) is needed to produce just 1 litre (1.8 pt) of petrol.

Paper making

As much as 1 litre (1.8 pt) of water is used to make each A4 sheet of paper you write upon. Paper making begins with wood chips being broken down into fibres by various stages of washing, heating, and treating. Floating wood fibres are then caught on a perforated flat surface and the water is squeezed out to leave a large sheet of paper.

Sand blasting

Water blasted at high pressure has tremendous cutting power. If particles of hard sand or gemstones (called "abrasives") are mixed with this water, the spray can cut like a knife or chisel. Here, a water and abrasive jet is being blasted out to cut through sandstone rock.

Waste water

All industries produce waste water, which contains chemicals that can be harmful to wildlife and people. This waste water is usually treated before it can be released safely into the environment. Here, waste water from a chemical plant is being emptied onto a beach.

Silk dyeing

These colourful Indian saris are made of silk. The fibres are first washed, untangled, and spun using large amounts of water, then they are woven into cloth. More water is involved in dyeing, printing, and washing the silk before it is cut and sewn into clothing.

Our rivers and seas are becoming more polluted – by people and industries releasing high levels of harmful substances into the environment. Almost everything we spill, throw away, burn, or bury will eventually find its way to the sea. Even fumes that float as air particles finally settle on water, while falling rain can carry pollution out of the air or off the land.

Dirty water

Too many nutrients

This river in Thailand is rich in nutrients, such as nitrates and phosphates, that have been washed into the water from fields. People have also put untreated sewage into the river. The nutrient-rich water has caused microscopic plants called phytoplankton to bloom, staining the river green. But few other organisms can survive in these conditions, and microbes from the sewage are a health hazard.

Waste from mines

This copper mine emptied its polluted waste water into a river. The waste water is laden with particles of rock, called sediment, along with traces of copper and other heavy metals. The particles smother any water-living plants and small animals, and the heavy metals can be poisonous to plants and wildlife. In most developed countries, this type of pollution is now illegal.

Tainted waters

In November 2002, the oil tanker "Prestige" broke up and sank off the coast of Spain. More than half the ship's cargo of fuel oil spilled into the Atlantic Ocean. Fuel oil contains poisonous substances that can be taken in by plankton and fish, then passed on to any creatures that eat them. After this spill, all local fishing had to be halted.

Threatened whales

Harmful chemicals in the St Lawrence River, Canada, are threatening the local population of beluga (white) whales. Heavy metals and pesticides wash or empty into the river and are taken in by the fish and shellfish on which the belugas feed. When these substances get into the whales' tissues, they can cause cancers and other life-threatening conditions.

Clean-up operation

It is better to prevent pollution in the first place, rather than clean up after it has happened. Here, an oil spill is being contained within floating booms before it is sucked up onto a vessel. However, in most cases of pollution there is no way of retrieving harmful substances once they have made their way into the environment.

Flood and

Too much or too little water can have devastating consequences. When rivers burst their banks, or a tsunami hits, the resulting floods can sweep away buildings, crops, cattle, and people. At the other extreme, a temporary shortage of water can kill crops and cattle. During droughts in poorer countries, people die from lack of food and clean water. The extent to which people are affected by flood or drought depends on local climate and the resources available to combat the effects.

Monsoon floods

In many Asian countries, from India to Japan, floods happen every year. In summer, monsoon winds bring torrential rain that drenches towns and cities. The areas of highest flood risk lie around the mouths of mighty rivers such as the Ganges and Yangtze.

Hurricane hits

In some places, floods are such rare events that emergency services are not prepared. On 29th August, 2005, Hurricane Katrina slammed into the US city of New Orleans. It created a storm surge nearly 9 m (30 ft) high. The water overwhelmed the levees (large embankments) built to protect the city from floods. Helicopters dropped sandbags in an effort to seal the break.

drought

Flood & drought facts

3 million
people a year lose homes in floods

13 m (43 ft)
of rain a year in Lloro, Columbia, makes it the wettest place on Earth

1 in 12
people is chronically short of water

30%
of the world's land may face drought by the end of this century

On dry land

A water shortage occurs regularly in many places, including southeast Australia, southern California in the USA, and Sudan in Africa. A slight shift in air circulation is all it takes for the moisture-laden winds that arrive one year not to return the next. While rich countries make up for this by bringing in water from other parts of the country, in poorer countries a water shortage can mean huge loss of life.

Desert advances

The spread of desert into surrounding farmland is known as desertification, and it is a growing problem. Although this is partly due to global climate change, a lack of moisture-rich vegetation is also to blame. When cattle overgraze or farmers burn vegetation, desertification speeds up. Here in China, workers are planting suitable crops to help bind the soil.

NORTH AMERICA

ASIA

EUROPE

Pacific Ocean

Atlantic Ocean

AFRICA

Annual precipitation

Less than 500 mm (20 in)

500–2,000 mm (20–80 in)

More than 2,000 mm (80 in)

SOUTH AMERICA

Indian Ocean

AUSTRALASIA

Precipitation around the world

Average precipitation varies greatly, as this map shows. Near the coast, where moist winds blow, rainfall is often high. Conditions are drier inland – such as in North America and Asia. Near the Equator, rising warm, moist air creates heavy rainfall. Where dry air descends, as in parts of South America, southern Africa, and Australia, there are deserts. These are places with less than 250 mm (10 in) of rain a year.

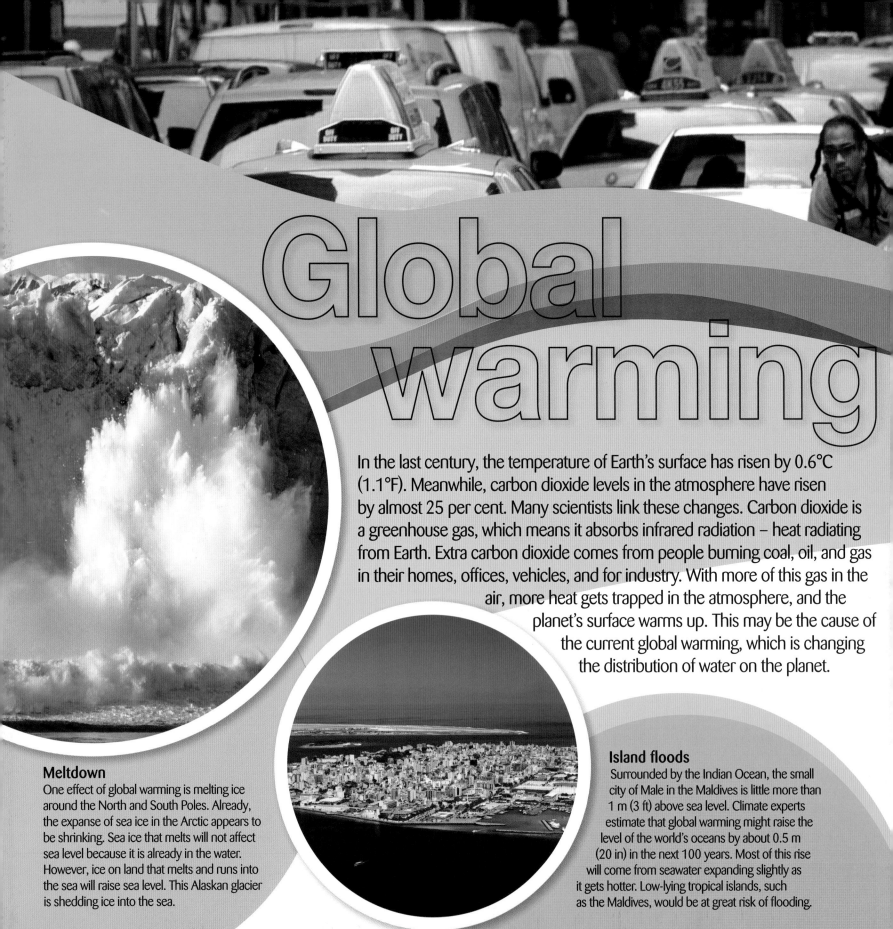

Global warming

In the last century, the temperature of Earth's surface has risen by 0.6°C (1.1°F). Meanwhile, carbon dioxide levels in the atmosphere have risen by almost 25 per cent. Many scientists link these changes. Carbon dioxide is a greenhouse gas, which means it absorbs infrared radiation – heat radiating from Earth. Extra carbon dioxide comes from people burning coal, oil, and gas in their homes, offices, vehicles, and for industry. With more of this gas in the air, more heat gets trapped in the atmosphere, and the planet's surface warms up. This may be the cause of the current global warming, which is changing the distribution of water on the planet.

Meltdown
One effect of global warming is melting ice around the North and South Poles. Already, the expanse of sea ice in the Arctic appears to be shrinking. Sea ice that melts will not affect sea level because it is already in the water. However, ice on land that melts and runs into the sea will raise sea level. This Alaskan glacier is shedding ice into the sea.

Island floods
Surrounded by the Indian Ocean, the small city of Male in the Maldives is little more than 1 m (3 ft) above sea level. Climate experts estimate that global warming might raise the level of the world's oceans by about 0.5 m (20 in) in the next 100 years. Most of this rise will come from seawater expanding slightly as it gets hotter. Low-lying tropical islands, such as the Maldives, would be at great risk of flooding.

Traffic pollution

These New York taxis are releasing carbon dioxide into the atmosphere through their exhausts. In the USA, about 33 per cent of carbon dioxide emissions come from cars burning petrol or diesel. Another 40 per cent comes from burning fossil fuels to generate electricity. One way to combat global warming would be to find alternatives to burning fossil fuels. This would help counter the rising levels of carbon dioxide in the atmosphere.

Weather alert

With global warming, weather across much of the world will become more unpredictable. Extreme weather, including hurricanes and snowstorms, such as this one in New York, USA, are expected to occur more often.

Pastures new

If global warming continues, parts of the world will become warmer and wetter, while others will turn cooler and drier. These changes will cause the distribution of animals to shift, as they relocate to the climates that suit them best. For example, swarms of locusts that currently eat crops in northwest Africa may move north into southern Europe and western Asia.

Crop failure

This maize crop in Texas, USA, is wilting from the heat of the Sun. Global warming will cause droughts (lack of water) in places where droughts do not currently occur. Farmers in such regions may have to grow different crops or cultivate special drought-resistant strains of the crops they grow at present.

The future

To face the future with some hope about water supplies, scientists and engineers are developing technologies that will make the best use of this essential resource. However, there are grave imbalances – many developed countries are wasteful, while some developing countries do not have enough water. People across the world will have to recycle and conserve water more efficiently than they do at present, if everyone is to get a fair share and the global environment is not put in peril.

Increased demands
As the world's population continues to rise, more people are chasing fewer natural resources. In many areas, fresh water for drinking, irrigating crops, and safe sanitation is becoming increasingly scarce.

Eyes in the sky
Satellites can relay crucial information to experts on the ground. In 2007, European scientists launch the first satellite that will measure the salinity (saltiness) of the sea surface. This ENVISAT satellite image of the Aral Sea shows how this giant lake has shrunk to a patchwork of smaller lakes.

Eden Project
This environmental complex in Cornwall, England, centres on a series of bubble-like greenhouses that grow plants from several climatic regions. Studying these plant communities helps scientists understand how water is used and recycled in nature. This, in turn, provides ideas for ways people can work in harmony with nature to maximize recycling and minimize wastage.

Ocean technology

Engineers are learning how to tap previously unused sources of water. Here, in the Mediterranean Sea, fresh water is being piped to the surface from a spring that is 36 m (118 ft) down on the seabed. The water flows naturally undergound from the mountainous Alps on mainland Europe. Passing ships can stop and collect the water.

Fish farming

Today, more than 30 per cent of the fish people eat is farmed in ponds or cages. This percentage will rise as people continue to overfish the open sea. With coastal waters becomingly increasingly overcrowded – largely due to recreation – technologies are being developed to locate fish farms further out to sea.

A world with safe water

In March 2005, the United Nations launched its Decade of Water for Life (2005–2015). At the moment about one person in every six worldwide has no access to safe drinking water. One of the aims of the campaign is to greatly improve this figure by helping communities to set up facilities for digging wells and pumping up water from aquifers.

Facts and figures

The amount of water that arrives on Earth each year, carried by comets and meteorites, is about the same amount that escapes back into space.

The Three Gorges Dam in China should protect about 300 million people from floods. However, two million people have had to move because of the lake that feeds the dam.

In some industrialized countries, about 30 per cent of the water used at home is flushed down the toilet.

In the USA, farm animals produce 130 times more solid and liquid waste than the human population.

Fruit and vegetables are mainly water – tomatoes are 95 per cent and apples are 85 per cent.

More than half the population of the USA relies on ground water for their water supplies.

Some Greek islands get their drinking water from ships that tow giant bags full of 2,000,000 litres (528,346 gal) of water.

In Namibia, Nepal, and Norway, more than 90 per cent of electricity is generated by hydroelectric dams.

A tap that drips once every 10 seconds wastes more than 1,000 litres (264 gal) of water a year.

When lightning strikes a tree, the water inside may boil, blowing the tree apart.

The World Health Organization estimates that three people a minute die due to unsafe water and poor sanitation. Most are children.

Today, more than 90 per cent of the world's glaciers are retreating due to global warming.

Canada has the longest marine coastline in the world.

The Ogallala Aquifer in the USA contains "fossil water" that is tens of thousands of years old.

One of the planet Jupiter's moons, Europa, may have giant oceans beneath its surface.

In the last 200 years, about half the world's wetlands have been lost, mainly to draining for agricultural use.

Most homes in the world do not have a tap for drinking water. The majority of people have to get their water from a community supply.

The amount of water on Earth has stayed roughly constant for millions, perhaps billions, of years.

When electricity is passed through water in a controlled process, it splits water into its basic elements – hydrogen and oxygen. These gases can be collected.

The water from the equivalent of 350,000,000 Olympic swimming pools evaporates from Earth's surface each day.

Each time you brush your teeth with the tap running it uses up to 7.5 litres (2 gal) of water.

In the UK, an average household spends less than 0.02 per cent of income on water. In Uganda a household spends more than 3 per cent, while in Tanzania, it is more than 5 per cent.

In developing countries, more than two-thirds of industrial waste water is dumped into the environment without being treated.

The roof of the building at Frankfurt Airport captures more than 15,000,000 litres (3,962,593 gal) of rain a year. This water supplies gardens, toilets, and other facilities.

The surface of Mars is marked with trenches, which may once have been rivers. The water on Mars today is frozen.

The Dead Sea is like a lake with no link to open sea. It is 415 m (1,362 ft) below sea level, the lowest body of water on Earth.

An oak tree transpires about 1,000 litres (264 gal) of water a day – the equivalent of three baths full of water.

In some rivers, such as China's Yellow River, so much water is used by people that the river runs dry before reaching the sea.

The human kidneys filter about 170 litres (300 pt) of blood for every litre of urine they produce.

Scientists calculate that if Earth had been 8 per cent nearer the Sun, life would not have evolved. It would have been too warm for liquid water.

If all the water in the Great Lakes was spread across the USA, the ground would be covered with 3 m (10 ft) of water.

The wettest 24 hours was on 16th March 1970, when 1.9 m (74 in) of rain fell on Reunion Island in the Indian Ocean.

In parts of China, India, and the USA, ground water is being used more quickly than it is being replaced. As a result, water tables are falling dramatically.

Australia is the world's driest inhabited continent with rainfall averaging only 455 mm (17.7 in) per year.

On 3rd September 1970, a hailstone weighing 0.77 kg (1lb 11 oz) fell in Kansas, USA.

About 80 per cent of the sickness and disease in developing countries is water-related.

Since 1957, the Aral Sea in Kazakhstan has shrunk in volume by two-thirds as its water has been used to irrigate land.

58

Timeline

From the earliest farmers who diverted water from rivers to feed their crops, right up to the engineers who design today's huge dams, people have been interested in exploring and controlling water. On this timeline you can track some of the most significant water-related events of the last 4 billion years.

c. 4 billion years ago
Earth's first oceans form – possibly a result of the cooling of hot gases from volcanoes.

c. 180 million years ago
All the world's landmasses are joined in one supercontinent, called Pangaea, surrounded by an ocean, called Panthalassa.

c. 9000 BCE
Farmers in Mesopotamia (modern-day Iraq) grow the first cereal crops using irrigation methods.

c. 4000 BCE
The ancient Egyptians are making large sea-going boats from woven papyrus reeds.

c. 600 BCE
The Romans are using underground mains sewers in their cities across Europe.

c. 550 BCE
Nebuchadnezzar of Babylon has a large dam built between the Tigris and Euphrates rivers, creating a giant lake.

3rd century BCE
Greek scientist Archimedes takes a bath and discovers that a body displaces its own volume in water.

2nd century BCE
Aqueducts are being widely used in the Roman Empire for carrying water above ground and across valleys.

1st century BCE
The Greek inventor and mathematician Hero of Alexandria builds a simple steam engine.

c. 980 AD
Chinese engineer Jiao Weiyo constructs a lock that allows a boat to move between different levels in a canal.

1674
English scientist Robert Boyle reports how temperature and pressure change with depth in the sea.

1687
English scientist Isaac Newton explains how the Moon's gravitational pull produces tides on Earth.

1712
Englishmen Thomas Newcomen and Thomas Savery build the first practical steam engine. It uses pistons and cylinders.

1742
Swede Anders Celsius develops the Celsius temperature scale, based on the freezing and boiling points of water.

1778
Englishman Joseph Bramah patents one of the earliest flushing toilets.

1783
Frenchmen Lavoisier and Laplace show that water is made from the elements hydrogen and oxygen.

1796
Frenchman Joseph Montgolfier invents a hydraulic ram – a system for raising water using the power of a waterfall.

1800
Englishmen William Nicholson and Anthony Carlisle use electricity to split water into hydrogen and oxygen gases.

1803
A lecturer in meteorology, British chemist Luke Howard invents names for clouds, such as cirrus and cumulus.

1805
Frenchman Joseph-Louis Gay-Lussac shows that water is made of two parts hydrogen to one part oxygen.

1829
Scotsman James Simpson develops a water purification system, using sand filters.

1854
English doctor John Snow traces an outbreak of cholera to a contaminated well, proving that it is spread in water.

1855
The first permit to bottle and sell mineral water is granted to Vittel Grande Source in France. Perrier follows in 1863.

1876
The Merchant Shipping Act requires all UK cargo ships to be marked with a Plimsoll line, beyond which they cannot be loaded.

1872–76
Scientists on board "HMS Challenger" carry out the world's first major expeditions to explore the ocean depths.

1882
A waterwheel on the Fox River in Wisconsin, USA, becomes the first commercial hydroelectric power generator.

1912
The British passenger ship "Titanic" strikes an iceberg and sinks in the North Atlantic Ocean, killing 1,517 people.

1921
Englishman Joseph Swan invents the modern electric kettle for boiling water.

1936
The Hoover Dam, the first gravity arch dam, is completed on the borders of Arizona and Nevada, USA.

1944
The world's longest water supply tunnel opens. It stretches 169 km (105 miles) from Rondout reservoir into New York, USA.

1951
British scientists locate the deepest point in the oceans. Situated in the Marianas Trench in the Pacific Ocean, it is 10,912 m (35,800 ft) deep.

1956
The world's largest glacier is discovered in Antarctica. The Lambert Glacier is 700 km (440 miles) long.

1958
US nuclear-powered submarine "Nautilus" passes right under the Arctic ice, proving that there is no land at the North Pole.

1960
Scientists in the bathyscaphe "Trieste" descend to the deepest point in the Marianas Trench.

1977
US scientists in the submersible "Alvin" discover deep-sea hydrothermal vents in the Pacific Ocean.

1978
NASA launches SEASAT, the first remote-sensing satellite with instruments to measure many features of the oceans.

1986
The world's largest tidal river barrier, the 9-km (5.6-miles) long Oosterscheldedam, opens in the Netherlands.

1989
The oil tanker "Exxon Valdez" strikes a reef off Alaska, USA and releases enough oil to fill 125 swimming pools.

1994
The Law of the Sea, governing how nations should use and safeguard the oceans, comes into force.

2004
On 26th December, a massive tsunami in the Indian Ocean causes the deaths of nearly 230,000 people.

2005
The world's largest desalination plant, for turning seawater into fresh water opens in Ashkelon, Israel.

2006
The world's first luxury underwater hotel, Hydropolis, is under construction off the coast of Dubai.

2007
The first satellite that measures the saltiness of the sea surface is to be launched by the European Space Agency.

2009
The Three Gorges Dam on China's Yangtze River, the world's largest dam, is due to become fully operational.

Glossary

Acid rain
Rain made more acidic by air pollution, especially from burning fossil fuels in homes, power stations, and motor vehicles.

Air mass
Body of air with fairly uniform temperature and humidity stretched over many miles within the lowest part of the atmosphere.

Aquifer
Region of rock or soil beneath the land surface that is saturated with water and through which water can move to supply wells.

Artesian well
Well that receives water under pressure from an aquifer. Water rises to a ground level without being pumped.

Atmosphere
Layer of gases surrounding Earth.

Atom
Smallest part of a chemical element.

Buoyancy
Upward pressure on a floating object produced by the water it pushes aside.

Cell
Tiny unit that makes up an animal or plant body. A cell contains a centre, called the nucleus, and has an outer boundary, the cell membrane. Most animals and plants contain millions of cells.

Climate
General pattern of weather in a specific region over many years.

Condensation
Process of a gas turning into a liquid, such as water vapour condensing into water droplets.

Convection
Vertical circulation of a liquid or gas due to warm regions rising and cool regions sinking.

Coral reef
Limestone rock produced in warm, shallow sea water by small animals called hard coral polyps.

Coriolis effect
Effect of Earth's rotation to turn a wind or ocean current. This effect turns ocean currents clockwise in the Northern Hemisphere and anticlockwise in the Southern Hemisphere.

Dark zone
Lower region in an ocean, deeper than 1,000 m (3,300 ft), where no sunlight reaches.

Delta
Plain formed by the mouth of a river depositing sediment.

Displacement
Mass of water pushed aside by an object floating, sinking, or settling in the water.

Dissolve
To make a substance disperse and disappear in a liquid.

Drought
An extended period of little or no rainfall.

Element
Single substance that cannot be split into other substances by normal chemical means.

Energy
Ability to cause an action. Energy is not destroyed, but it changes from one form to another.

Erosion
Processes by which rock or soil are loosened and transported by glaciers, rivers, wind, and waves.

Estuary
Where a river meets the sea and fresh water mixes with sea water.

Evaporation
Process of liquid turning into a gas (vapour).

Flood
Water flowing onto ground that is normally dry.

Floodplain
Area of flat land over which the lower river floods naturally.

Fossil fuel
Fuel such as coal, oil, or natural gas that forms from the remains of long-dead organisms.

Fresh water
Water low in dissolved salts. It is defined as water containing less than 0.1 per cent dissolved salts.

Front
Forward moving edge of an air mass, such as a cold or hot front.

Geyser
Vent in the ground from which erupts volcanically heated water and steam.

Glacier
Large mass of snow and ice on land that builds up by repeated snowfalls. It flows slowly downhill under its own weight.

Global warming
Gradual increase in the average temperature across the world.

Gravitational attraction
Force of attraction between large masses. Heavier masses have greater gravitational attraction.

Greenhouse effect
Trapping of infrared radiation from Earth's surface by greenhouse gases in the atmosphere, producing a warming effect.

Greenhouse gas
Gas that absorbs infrared radiation, so trapping heat in the atmosphere. Carbon dioxide, methane, and water vapour are greenhouse gases.

Ground water
Water lying in soil or rock that may seep through it. Ground water supplies wells and springs.

Gyre
Large circular system of currents in an ocean.

Hard water
Fresh water that contains high levels of dissolved calcium and magnesium.

Humidity
Amount of water vapour in the air. The greater the humidity, the higher the water vapour content.

Hurricane
Violent, spiralling tropical storm with wind speeds in excess of 119 km/h (74 mph).

Hydrogen bond
Force of attraction between water molecules.

Hydrothermal vent
Seabed opening that releases volcanically heated water.

Ice age
Cold period in Earth's history when glaciers and ice sheets covered much of the land. The most recent ice age ended about 15,000 years ago.

Ice sheet
Large, thick layer of ice covering a landmass. Ice sheets cover most of Greenland and Antarctica.

Irrigation
System for supplying farmland with water by channels or pipes.

Levee
Raised bank along the lower reaches of a river, built from sediment deposited during floods.

Meteorite
A rock that falls from space and strikes the Earth.

Micro-organisms (microbes)
Microscopic organisms.

Mineral
Substance that is found in rock and may dissolve in water.

Molecule
Smallest amount of a substance with the properties of that substance. It normally consists of two or more atoms held together by chemical bonds, as in water (H_2O).

Monsoon
Seasonal winds that blow across southern and eastern Asia. Summer monsoon winds bring heavy rains from moist air above the Indian and Pacific Oceans.

Nutrients
These are substances such as nitrate and phosphate that plants need supplied in order to grow.

Ocean current
Major flow of seawater. Surface currents are normally driven by winds or temperature differences, with warm sea water rising and cool sea water sinking.

Organism
A living thing.

Photosynthesis
Process by which plants, and plant-like micro-organisms, make food by trapping sunlight.

Phytoplankton
Plant-like micro-organisms that live in the sea and in fresh water.

Plankton
Organisms that float in the sea, lakes, or slow rivers and get pushed along by currents.

Pollution
People releasing substances, or factors such as heat or sound, into the environment at levels that could be harmful to wildlife.

Precipitation
Water falling or settling from the air onto land or sea. Rain, snow, sleet, hail, frost, and dew are types of precipitation.

Salt
Substance commonly formed by the reaction between an acid and an alkali or an acid and a metal. The most common salt is sodium chloride, which goes on food and is the main type of salt found in sea water.

Saltwater
Water that contains high levels of dissolved salts. Saltwater is found in the sea and some inland lakes.

Satellite
Object that orbits a planet. Artificial remote-sensing satellites orbit Earth monitoring the weather and land and sea conditions.

Sea
Water in an ocean. It is also the name for part of an ocean, such as the Caribbean Sea.

Sea ice
Ice forming as sea water freezes.

Sea wave
Vertical disturbance that travels along the sea surface. Most sea waves are wind driven. The largest waves (tsunamis) come from earthquakes, volcanoes, landslides, or meteorites.

Sediment
Loose material eroded from the land and deposited elsewhere.

Sewer
System of underground pipes that carry waste water away from houses, businesses, factories, and to water treatment works.

Soft water
Fresh water that contains low levels of dissolved calcium and magnesium.

Stalactite
Hanging, icicle-like structure made of calcium carbonate.

Stalagmite
Rising, candle-like structure made of calcium carbonate.

Stomata (stomatal pores)
Openings on the stem and leaves of plants. Water vapour escapes through stomata and other gases enter and leave through them.

Sunlit zone
Upper region in an ocean, defined as shallower than 200 m (660 ft). Here, enough sunlight reaches the plants and plant-like micro-organisms for photosynthesis.

Surface tension
Attraction between water molecules at water's surface.

Synovial fluid
Fluid that lubricates human joints, reducing wear and tear on bones.

Tide
Rise and fall of sea water produced by the gravitational attraction of the Moon and the Sun.

Transpiration
Loss of water from plants by evaporation.

Tsunami (harbour wave)
Large, fast-moving wave, or series of waves, that moves across the ocean. It is created by the disturbance from an earthquake, volcanic eruption, or large mass striking the water surface.

Twilight zone
Region in an ocean, at a depth between 200 m (660 ft) and 1,000 m (3,300 ft). Sunlight reaches this zone but not enough for plants or plant-like micro-organisms to photosynthesize.

Waste water
Water that has been used in homes, businesses, or industry.

Water cycle
Constant cycling of water between sea, air, and land. It involves evaporation, condensation, precipitation, and percolation.

Water table
Level below which soil or rock is saturated with ground water.

Weathering
Breakdown of rocks by physical, chemical, and biological processes at or near Earth's surface.

Zooplankton
Drifting animals and animal-like micro-organisms that live in the sea and fresh water.

Index

Credits

The publisher would like to thank the following for their kind permission to reproduce their photographs:

Abbreviations: a=above; b=below/bottom; c=centre; f=far; l=left; r=right; t=top)

2 John Shultis (www.johnshultis.com). 4 Alamy Images: ImageState (cl). **Corbis**: Royalty-Free (c). **Getty Images**: Ezio Geneletti (cr). **Science Photo Library**: Clive Freeman / Biosym Technologies (bl, bc, br). **5 Getty Images**: Richard H. Johnston (l). **NASA**: NASA (tl). **6 Getty Images**: Sakis Papadopoulos (cr). NASA: (tr). **Science Photo Library**: Matthew Oldfield / Scubazoo (br). **US Geological Survey**: Game McGimsey (fcl). **8 Photoshot / NHPA**: (c). **Science Photo Library**: David Nunuk (l); Peter Scoones (r). **9 Steven Bennett**: (crb). **Wikimedia Commons**: (clb).**10 Corbis**: Ralph A. Clevenger (cl). **Getty Images**: Joanna McCarthy (c); RGK Photography (br). **10-11 National Geographic Image Collection**: Maria Stenzel (cb).**11 Corbis**: Visuals Unlimited (tr). **Getty Images**: Jeff Spielman (cla); Jamie Squire (cr). **National Geographic Image Collection**: Maria Stenzel (tl). **Science Photo Library**: British Antarctic Survey (bc). **12 Corbis**: Theo Allofs/Zefa (tl). **Science Photo Library**: Jeremy Burgess (bl); Eye of Science (cr).**13 Science Photo Library**: Jeremy Burgess (c); Steve Gschmeissner (bl). **14 NASA**: Jeff Schmaltz (bl). **Science Photo Library**: Juergen Berger (br); Steve Gschmeissner (tr). **14-15 Alamy Images**: Jane Burton (c).**15 SeaPics.com**: (cr, tr). **16 Still Pictures**: Arnold Newman (t). **16-17 OSF / photolibrary**: Michael Fogden (b). **17 Science Photo Library**: Nature's images (tl); Ria Novosti (tr); Bjorn Svensson (tc). **18 Corbis**: Louise Gubb (c); Layne Kennedy (cl); Christophe Loviny (cr); Olivier Matthys / epa (fcl). **19 Corbis**: Yann Arthus Bertrand (c); **NASA** (cr); Sandy Stockwell (fcl); Raimundo Valentim (cl). **20 Getty Images**: Gary Bell (l). **22 Science Photo Library**: Andrew J. Martinez (br). **23 Getty Images**: John Bilderback (br); Martin Harvey (cr). **Science Photo Library**: Andrew J. Martinez (bl). **24 Alamy Images**: David South (l). Corbis: David Muench (r). **25 Alamy Images**: nagelestock.com (tl). Getty Images: Jerry Alexander (br); Kristian Maak (tr). **27 Corbis**: Jim Reed (c). **NOAA**: (br). **29 Flagstaffotos**: Peter Firus (c). http://sl.**wikipedia.org**: moo@fp.chu.jp (bl). **Wikimedia Commons**:

pfctdayelise (br). **30 Corbis**: Chinch Gryniewicz / Ecoscene (bl); Roy Morsch (tl). **31 Corbis**: Frans Lanting (br). **Marcelle Dulude**: (cr). **Saskia van Lijnschooten**: (tr). **37 Science Photo Library**: CNRI (crb); Susumu Nishinaga (cra). **38 Corbis**: Bettmann (bl). **38-39 US Department of Interior (www.usbr.gov). 39 Alamy Images**: David Hoffman Photo Library (br); Doug Houghton (cr). Flickr / Ingrid Koehler: London Looks (tr). **40-41 Getty Images**: Hans Strand (c). **41 Getty Images**: Alexander Stewart (tl); Penny Tweedie (bl). **42 Science Photo Library: NIAID / CDC** (br). **42-43 Corbis**: Anna Clopet. **43 Alamy Images**: Dennis Pedersen (tr). **Corbis**: Viviane Moos (br). **Science Photo Library**: Peter Menzel (cra). **44 Corbis**: David Forman / Eye Ubiquitous (tl); Steve Kaufman (tr). **45 Corbis**: Gina Glover (tl). **Science Photo Library**: Simon Fraser (br). **46 Corbis**: Eberhard Streichan / Zefa. **47 Corbis**: Jeremy Horner (br); Eberhard Streichan / Zefa (tl). **Science Photo Library**: Robert Brook (cl); Pascal Goetgheluck (cr); Geoff Tompkinson (tr). **48 Alamy Images**: Kevin Lang (bl). Corbis: Lowell Goergia (br). **48-49 Corbis**: EPA (t). **49 Getty Images**: Norbert Rosing (bl); Mike Simons (br). **50 Corbis**: Smiley N. Pool / Dallas Morning News (tr). **Getty Images**: Martin Puddy (t). **51 Corbis**: Michael Reynolds / epa (c). **Getty Images**: Martin Mawson (t). **52 Getty Images**: Tom Bean (cl). http://sl.wikipedia.org: (br). **53 Corbis**: Reuters (cr). **Michael Donohoe / Flickr**: (cl). **Science Photo Library**: Mike Boyatt / Agstock (bl). **54 European Space Agency**: (tr). **54-55 Juergen Matern**: (b). **55 Science Photo Library**: Alexis Rosenfeld (tl). **UNESCO**: Tang Chhin (cr)

Jacket images: Front: **Alamy Images**: Foodfolio t; **Saskia van Lijnschooten**: b. Back: **Pete Atkinson (www.peteatkinson. com)**: bl; **Corbis**: Zefa tl; **Getty Images**: Thierry Dosogne cr; **NASA**: cl; **Science Photo Library**: Eye of Science br

All other images © Dorling Kindersley
For further information see: **www.dkimages.com**

Dorling Kindersley would like to thank:
Hazel Beynon for proofreading; Lynn Bresler for the index; Jane Thomas for additional design.